Penguin Special
Community Decay

Jon Rowland was educated at the Architectural Association School of
Architecture in London. He has worked on slum-clearance projects in
the East End, and he was involved in the germination of a project
for portable operating theatres for use in disasters by the Red Cross
and the World Health Organization. He has also worked on building
systems for the less industrialized countries and participated in a
conference in Geneva on the strategy of global planning. He is at
present researching into urbanization and re-use techniques.

JON
ROWLAND

PENGUIN BOOKS

COMMUNITY
DECAY

Penguin Books Ltd, Harmondsworth,
Middlesex, England
Penguin Books Inc., 7110 Ambassador Road,
Baltimore, Maryland 21207, U.S.A.
Penguin Books Australia Ltd, Ringwood,
Victoria, Australia

First published 1973

Made and printed in Great Britain by
Fletcher & Son Ltd, Norwich
Set in Monotype Univers

I would like to thank:
Annie
Dalibor
David
Elinor
Keith
Martin
Mike
and, of course, my parents

Contents

1. Preface

This book deals with the present isolation and decay of a 'non-community' in part of North London's urban core. It is only fair to put it in its correct perspective. The main part of the book is taken up with a series of surveys, case studies and suggested conclusions to a number of problems in North Islington. It is preceded by a very generalized preamble, setting out the problems at a more universal level. Each paragraph has had books written about the subject it deals with, so that it is only meant as an outline to those who might be later prompted to take a much deeper look at some of the general trends affecting everybody today.

July 1970

2. Prologue

The Apollo missions were scientifically and economically dubious. But they communicated information of world-wide consequences not for the future of man on other planets but for his existence on this planet. Apollo showed for all to see, both on T.V. and in print, that the earth was finite – its resources were finite, its mass was finite, its air was finite. The immediate result was an outburst of interest in ecology and anti-pollution drives. But this finiteness has had a far subtler and deeper-grained effect. Who is going to control the existing resources? I am, unfortunately, not a great believer in man's essential good sense and I see various pressures from the past, exacerbated to the point of conflict, for the reason of survival of the fittest.

This Darwinian implication extends not only to the economic conflict between the 'developed' and 'lesser-developed' nations but also the 'haves' and 'have-nots' within the industrial societies. Because it will be the industrial societies, whether it be the U.S. or U.S.S.R., that will endeavour to control the sources of revenue for their own uses; the U.S. and U.S.S.R. have world control of economic investments, and subtle imperialism. Europe hangs on to its former protectorates by control of resource outlets and financial arrangements. It is this realization of finiteness that has led to the scrabble for all resources.

But this Darwinian principle applies not only on a world level, but on a very local level. A battle of survival is beginning within the industrial cities. One could be very crude and say that this is not only in economic terms but also in terms of human life, because as this realization of finiteness progresses, then the probability of conflict rises. The increase in automation and cybernetically controlled industry contributes to the insecurity of those adversely affected. The increase in bureaucratization of authority alienates those at the 'grass roots' level. The computing of information will mean a 'displacement' of man in relation to his perception of reality.

Those without access, or knowledge of access, to the resources will be dispossessed from society as a whole. What becomes of them? – who knows; they could be paid off, they could very easily starve – contrary to the optimism of Buckminster Fuller – either way they will have no part to play in society; they will be unable to take part in leisure activities, use the educational resources; they will be divorced from the communications revolution. They will become totally alienated. When I say they *will* be, implying that this is in the future, I mean that the numbers who are already in this situation – and there are many – will multiply considerably. By how much is a political question. The situation will get worse; maybe only to the point where there will still be a large enough buying public and working people to consume the products that are automatically and cybernetically manufactured, and maybe not. The recognition of the concept of finiteness is accompanied by the closing of ranks of all involved in the struggle. Those disagreeing with the existing order do so more violently. Those maintaining the status quo consolidate. Threats to security are discriminated against. There is a return to nationalism, tribalism and scapegoatism. The quest for identification with the secure tenets of industrial civilization will intensify. Economically the affluent worker class will grow, and as is already happening, merge with the middle class – aspiring to its ideals of leisure, education, security and fantasy; but the gap will widen between those who have the money and opportunities and those who don't, those who have skilled jobs and those who are untrained and unskilled.

Out of these conditions the losers emerge. Those in the economic ghettoes and the 'deprived' areas, the dispossessed, the alienated, the 'no-chance people'.

3. General Situation

Alienation is essentially experiencing the world
and oneself passively, receptively, as the
subject separated from the object.

FAUNCE

Social Alienation

Historically, the preparations for the battle for survival can be
seen to have begun with the collapse of the medieval social
system and eighteenth-century humanitarianism which was
helped by the emergence of popular evangelical protestantism.
Starting on a street-action level, it caused repercussions within
the ruling elite that affect us today. With formal religion
emphasizing the rationality of Christianity, rather than setting
itself against the existing social order, a number of evangelists
who believed that the social pyramid did not exist before, in
front of God, began preaching around the industrial areas. Their
preachings emphasized a need for the 'saving' of all men, and
promised equality of souls before God. This puritanism greatly
appealed to the middle classes with their striving for material
equality and respectability. All this led to a renewal of 'self-
discipline', the effects of which were felt through the factories,
with the workers somewhat on the receiving end. In this religious
revival, the rich were not left out. Good causes to save souls
through religio-political action and charities, increased. The
freeing of slaves and prohibition of cruelty to children were
among the more fashionable causes. This helped the
strengthening and revitalizing of personal standards of morality.
Yet there was no effort to do away with social distinctions,
rather to justify them by a new sort of righteousness. Thus the
nouveaux riches and middle classes rigidly held to the new
righteousness and continued to rise within their society. It was
a duty to work, everyone had their place in the hierarchy; to be
wealthy was good, and to be poor was sinful. The workers had
to content themselves with a social pyramid in another world

and when the promises of equality failed to come about fewer were prepared to believe in eternal life. Death meant a total end, what M. B. Scott calls 'annihilation of self'. Work, purportedly a 'creative challenge', helped allay these fears.

However, work became no longer tolerable. It was now necessary to survive at work in order to survive. New attitudes were required for urban living. Men had to work at the machines' pace. Time was measured in hours and pieces, no longer in terms of seasons or years. Life was regulated by the factory and the imposition of penalties and work rules, due to the demands of the machinery. The Guild system broke down and its protection was lost. The new capitalism undermined local autonomy and local self-sufficiency and depersonalized the existing socio-economic structure. Man was left with nothing but a sense of incongruity at his 'non-living' life. He recognised his total end. He became 'estranged' from the product of his own hand, no longer experiencing himself as the 'acting agent' in his world. The 'self-fulfilment' of creative work grew more and more distant with increasing mechanization. The 'new' individualism that evolved with the 'protestant ethic' created new kinds of dependencies. The growth of freedom away from direct outside powers blinded men to their inner restraints and conditioned adjustments, and was replaced by nebulous 'public opinion' and behaviour pressures. Thus for every new outer freedom gained, an old inner freedom was given in exchange.

With the apex of the social pyramid in control of education, the church, culture media and wealth, and therefore goodness, there was positive pressure for the working class to imitate these values and psychologically identify themselves with their aspirations. Those who were successful moved upward in the socio-economic hierarchy. Those remaining withdrew both sociologically and psychologically, growing more and more 'distant' from 'society's norms'.

In the twentieth century an aggrieved middle section of the pyramid, not content with its educational and cultural lot, broke down the old upper-class monopoly of culture. 'Business' realized the potential profit in producing mass culture products. Communications techniques were continuously improved, and meant a wider market for these products. Commodities flooded all levels of society, which in due course came to demand more trivial and 'comfortable' products until it was no longer being exploited but was actively choosing its own total end. Meanwhile, the working man who manufactures these products is becoming alienated from the process of work, from the product of work, from his fellow workers, and finally from himself. He sells his labour as a commodity. He is a cog in a world-wide economic machine to serve a purpose outside himself. Fromm suggests that this readiness to submit oneself to extra-human needs was actually prepared by the 'protestant ethic'. Lutheran and Calvinist teachings laid the ground for this redevelopment, by breaking the spiritual structure of an earlier socio-economic framework and by teaching man that work activity had to further aims outside his own needs, so losing its pleasurability and becoming a duty.

The transformation of the concrete form of exchange, personal dealings and rewards, to the abstract concerns of millions of customers worth millions of pounds, reinforced the role of man as a cog. He became dependent on something, not someone, to pay, hire, or sack him. This impersonality shifted his spiritual focus from intrinsic to extrinsic values, whether they were wages or securities. Today all work is in terms of reward money. The worker is not related to the concrete product as a whole. The reward money increased the abstract quality of work so that eventually everything is experienced as a commodity, an embodiment of some exchange value system, not only while being bought or sold, but in our attitude towards it. This makes it easier to grasp the concept of expendability of commodities, both in terms of objects and people. People are now commodities, worth so much and quantifiable in abstract terms like statistics, so that reality is no longer present. 'Things' have become so unwieldy that we are unable to deal with them within a human scale of reference. The increasing availability of world-wide information in McLuhan's 'global village' means, of necessity, a surfeit of overstated and oversimplified visual and aural images, that have anaesthetized many of the feelings that would have been felt. The armchair experiences and responses that we feel or demonstrate are someone else's abstractions of an estranging medium.

Alienation is a manner of living by which a person experiences himself as an outsider. He is outside the fold of society's norms both physically, economically and socially. He is estranged from himself. He is not the centre of his world, nor the creator of his acts; out of touch with himself, out of touch with others. He feels himself as a 'thing', and is experienced by others as a commodity. His potential is ignored; after all a product is only a 'present thing', its uses are only in terms of present policies, to be manipulated or discarded according to future decisions outside himself. His aim is to sell himself successfully on the market and his own personal sense of value depends on his success. Sometimes his failure to elicit approval in relation to others can force him to retreat to his basic securities to maintain his self esteem and compensate for insecurity and anxiety. This 'Wendy House' syndrome covers up what he thinks are his inadequacies and helps him feel consciously secure. The parameters of his value-system tend to become vague and he perhaps lacks a commitment to an ultimate goal or direction. Indeed the values he is striving for may not be his, the methods of attaining them may be in other hands and the tools by which he can attain these values are often beyond his means, perhaps because of his physical, educational or working environment; these environments may be beyond his control. Thus if a man wants to become rich he can either gamble, sell himself well, although to do this he has to have at his command at least similar facilities and opportunities to those he is trying to emulate; or he can go outside the rules of society to obtain money in a way that society will condemn as illegal. So basically everything is stacked against him. The rules of the game are someone else's, and the further down the still-existing Victorian socio-economic pyramid he is, the fewer the tools at his disposal to enable him to realize his potential.

Among the tools of a man's behaviour at work are the ability to cope with the physical and economic environment, his expectations relating to his job, and the content and meaning of change for him. In some cases technological change is more difficult to accept. If he fails, even at being a commodity, and withdraws to his basic securities, then when the area of industry he is working for disintegrates, these securities become greater in importance. If the area declines, becoming 'deprived' or 'depressed', factories may close and work opportunities may lessen; automation or mechanization may all help to create a manpower 'mobility'. Most advocators of mobility (i.e. those not affected) would encourage modernization and the new definition of jobs and organizations which enable, in theory, great manpower movements. Those affected base their insecurity on a traditional reference system, a real fear of unemployment and movement from their roots. Whereas many aspirants tend to be favourably disposed to modernization and technological mobility, and are even prepared to be geographically mobile if more of their aspirations can be fulfilled, the unemployed worker tends to be less mobile, if at all, and unwilling or unable to leave his traditional base, not necessarily for 'positive' reasons, but more because of his 'negative' position which ensures even fewer employment opportunities. This, of course, depends on a system that allows free mobility of labour from 'depressed' to 'vital' areas. Technological change, with all its expectations, is perhaps more easily accepted the more the individual already participates in the 'modern consumption norms' or the higher his socio-economic level. Thus any aspirer has to accept higher work and social mobility and therefore higher wages to bring about a 'positive' change of life, breaking with existing norms and giving access to new values. The tendency is to become more committed to these new values and norms, more concerned over budgeting, planning and seeing the future in terms of children. The gap widens between the stable employed man, with all his aspirations, and the partially employed and unemployed man with his continued adherence to traditional values, who through his passive mobility becomes politically and geographically more contained, and in the end more 'containable' within his area.

Other factors affecting this situation can be seen. A report by the International Labour Office shows that recruiting of managers is no longer made from 'below', and far from loosening up democratically, the system of labour is becoming feudalistic. Within the employment area, the possibilities of social advancement offered by work are decreasing and tending to disappear. So the subordinated worker does not give his best energies because, after all, he has no initiative in his work, the choice of tools and methods is decided without him and he only has passively to follow the instructions. He does not participate in control of these methods, nor in the product and especially not in the profit, and any attempt at personal decision-making would disturb the whole production process. He is barred from higher employment by lack of sufficient knowledge and training and, what's more, is given little or no means of acquiring it. This applies to workers of any collar colour, since personal gratification as a result of work, and as an end in itself, and also as a result of products of one's efforts, is not a feeling enjoyed by many. As H. Swados summed it up in his book *The Myth of the Happy Worker*:

The worker's attitude towards his work is generally compounded by hatred, shame and resignation . . . They know that there is a difference between working with your back and working with your behind . . . They know that they work harder than the middle-class for less money . . . Nor is it simply . . . status hunger, that makes a man hate work that is mindless, endless, stupefying, sweaty, filthy, noisy, exhausting, insecure in its prospects, and practically without hope of advancement.

The plain truth is that factory work is degrading. It is degrading to any man who ever dreams of doing something worthwhile in his life; and it is about time we faced the fact.

At the same time, there has been a continual break-down of jobs, with increasing specialization, such that everyone knows his job activity but is not involved in the whole entity. Thus a worker is only likely to be manipulating a small nut or bolt without much concept of his part in the production-line nor of the end-product. Anyone can properly manipulate any one sector of a job, but reason can develop only if man's total perception is geared to the whole, and if he can deal with observable and manageable entities. The narrow and specialized jobs of industrialization can lead to 'alienation', especially when basic emotional desire is frustrated.

Work is not necessarily the only or even the primary area for 'self-realization', but the continued routinization of actions can repress any awareness of the basic problems of human existence. Ego involvement can withdraw from an activity of work that offers little prospect for 'self-realization' or 'self-esteem maintenance'. This may be an adaptive, rather than an inflexible response to the situation and could lead to a redefinition of personal aims and alternatives. As we have seen, the most devastating instance of this spirit of alienation is the individual's relationship to his own self. The repetitive thoughtlessness, the lack of control, creativeness or meaning lead to a physical sense of apathy as well as a social 'alienation' that turns to destructiveness and ultimately psychic regression.

But it is not only the person who, because of the routine of his work, has lost much of his 'self-identity', but more so those who have become 'isolated' from work, education, and housing systems, through no fault of their own but purely by 'force of circumstances' i.e. outside control. It is the unemployed and partially unemployed man, the unskilled man, who has not been 'fortunate' enough to have had an education outside an Educational Priority Area, or has not been 'fortunate' enough to have succeeded in the council housing listings, who has become 'alienated' from 'society'. With more than one million unemployed at present, eleven million people on or below the Ministry of Social Security's minimum income bread line, two million houses unfit for human habitation, what was an 'unimportant situation' a few years ago is increasingly urgent now ; it is these people who will affect any 'counter culture' in the near future, and not those who voluntarily opt out. Those on the higher reaches of the 'pyramid' want to keep the situation as it is. It is definitely in their interests to play the games of 'pretence of education, welfare programmes and urban renewal' using their own dice (loaded of course) and rules.

Automation

In factory automation, those affected first are those on the 'work bench', the unskilled and semi-skilled people. Those in control are affected last. In office automation, mechanization of information-processing is rapidly taking place. Most computers today perform a processing function and are not part of a technologically integrated system, which might lead to an eventual elimination of the peripheral processing operations now being carried out by the equivalent unskilled and semi-skilled men and women. When primary stage automation is completed, man will have begun to lose his significance as a worker.

Between 1940–55 the growth rate in automated industries was fast, but slowed down in the period to 1970, despite the pressure from industry to push ahead. With government investment in British research and technology, the rate of change is due to increase during the next five to ten years. The impact on labour-intensive industries, where labour costs are high in relation to the total costs of production, is expected to be 'sharp'. Previously capital-intensive industries which were affected by technological change tended to expand. This did not necessarily lead to any 'technological unemployment', in fact, in some cases the development led to increased employment in 'spin-off' industries. In 1969 the T.U.C. predicted that any repercussions on employment were likely to be less in these industries than those resulting from continuing older, less efficient and more costly methods of production; but the pressure operating between mechanized and automated industries is producing an employment vacuum. Those with no skills are caught in it. Industry is increasingly conglomerating and merging, to maintain the efficiency of an old production system. This means the closing down of many factories with nothing to take their place. It is known that when an old works closes down a new project worth several times its value is necessary to maintain the same number of jobs; this also assumes that those controlling the new works wish to stay within the area or, as is becoming increasingly common, to decentralize, thus leaving the area with less employment potential than was previously there.

So far, technological change has accelerated (albeit slowly) but there are indications of discontinuity with past rates. The emergence of the machine that replaces the skill of man has many implications. Instead of man's 'skill' and machines' 'power' (which is the situation today) the circumstances will alter to machines' 'skill' and machines' 'power'. The effect of this may decrease labour divisions in a production process from which direct human involvement has been eliminated and reduce the variety and numbers of tasks to be performed, so that machine monitoring and maintenance will be the remaining functions. The maintenance work will be of a highly skilled, mechanical, hydraulic and electrical nature, skills thus reducing specialization, but this, of course, does not necessarily mean an upgrading of the status of those involved in this maintenance. It has been predicted that future production systems may come closer to satisfying most demands for goods and services, with the major goals of post-industrial society shifting towards non-economic interests; but perhaps this social impact will only affect those who are part of the 'professional/technician/ technocrat group'. Those who are unable to get or take on 'broader responsibility' jobs or maintenance skills, become 'technologically unemployed', with a reduction in employment opportunities and a reversal into a 'vicious circle of poverty'.

All this technological progress has led to a change in hierarchical structure. It differentiates the potentially integrative effect of 'broader responsibility' work, into a bureaucratic elite, with technicians and the skilled at a lower hierarchical level, followed by 'organized workers', and, on the lowest rung, the jobless (those whose function is too menial even for automation).

With vast city growth in the late nineteenth and early twentieth centuries there was a great demand for those workers on the lowest hierarchical rung. The extensive divisions of labour ensured a continuous progression of occupational classifications, to be filled by men with little additional training, from lower job positions. The unskilled and semi-skilled manufacturing jobs thus became what Ginsberg calls 'the funnel' through which the unemployed were absorbed into the economic structure of the city. This centralizing effect soon came under strain due to a 'space locational demand'. The shortage of space in the inner London area led many firms to decentralize. This was due to various pressures; in some cases it was easier to supply wider markets and the increase in the share of durables in consumer spending meant that with more bulky products, more room was needed; in many cases 'spin-off' production became separated from central control.

The impact of decentralization on those involved in unskilled manufacturing jobs was very specific. Figures have been produced showing that the number of manufacturing jobs in the inner urban areas has declined. Service and government employment has made up for this in part but not entirely. The capability of the city to absorb the unskilled person is reduced, due both to lessening of employment opportunities in the manufacturing industries as a whole, and to the additional effects of technological advances which have reduced the relative number of unskilled jobs available. The narrowing of opportunities for the unskilled group has led to a 'serious imbalance' between existing manual jobs and the increasing demand for white collar employment. New clerical, technical and professional jobs were not able to be filled. The effect was to exacerbate the pressures on poor areas, thus forming economic ghettoes and starting the process of poverty, driving the middle classes out to the suburbs, which has the added effect of reducing even further the ability to provide amenities. For those who make it out of poor areas, there are employment opportunities at the bottom of the unskilled white-collar hierarchy. Thus service industries are now providing the 'absorption funnel' taking in the 'hard-to-employ' through the mechanization of the office. But the situation is just repeating itself, and, with computerized clerical work, what happened in the manufacturing industries is happening in the service industries, as the wheel of technological unemployment continues to revolve, with more drastic effects each time.

Soon, our society will have no place left for the unskilled man and even the skilled man will have to undertake repeated retraining to keep his skills from 'obsolescing'. The National Commission on Technology, Automation and Economic Progress stated that the output of the economy, and the aggregate demand to consume it, must grow more than 4 per cent per year to prevent unemployment from rising, and even faster if unemployment is to fall further. This implies a demand for technicians and skilled workers which is greater than the supply, while the supply of least skilled people is greater than the demand.

Two other aspects of unemployment are firstly the new entrants on the labour market, the young unskilled and drop-outs. In the U.S.A. in 1964 it was twice as difficult to get a job for a high school drop-out than for someone who had finished his education (young unskilled blacks found it twice as difficult as whites). This is not to suggest that the figures here are comparable, but secondary school unemployment is rising; in depressed areas the figures rise far more quickly. The other aspect is what is termed 'hidden unemployment'; those in high unemployment areas who have dropped out of the labour force, no longer looking for work but occasionally accepting it if available, and subsisting on social security, national assistance and child welfare maintenance. This group is entirely associated with the economic ghetto/twilight zone areas.

It is estimated that over 40 per cent of workers in the States are not full time, full year workers; these people are concentrated in the service industries. It is in these industries that a curious 'reverse commuting' takes place with those from deprived areas travelling quite far, just to be able to work. In many cases these jobs are decentralized and in the suburbs. It is likely that the urban cores will find it increasingly difficult to provide within their own geographical boundaries the kind of 'peripheral' and seasonal work (especially in summer when many young people work) to be able to supply adequate employment for the older casual and unskilled workers. These 'peripheral workers', engaged in what Whitelaw calls 'the murky sector' of the economy, who usually come from the twilight zones, help to increase the family income, and in some cases keep jobs that are uneconomic in order to be able to live. Eventually these workers tend to withdraw from the labour scene and help to increase the already present 'hidden unemployment' which is due to lack of information about jobs, lack of union support, lack of education and training and sometimes social security.

The potential use of automation is one of the main pressures in the battle for survival. The automated society, with its 'cottage industry' programmed by the individual in his house, machine-run factories and the potential release for leisure and education, is a utopian dream that will not exist for all. Its potential can only be completely realized by those who have both the education and technical knowledge to participate fully in an automated civilization. The group of people left out of this move towards an instant society are those still bounded by the environmental parameters of the deprived areas and those made redundant by increasing automation. The gap will widen between those participating and those alienated. One could be pessimistic about automation control, and see an Orwellian situation created, with the urban 'proles' cut off in ruined Inner London (perhaps very similar to what is already the situation in the U.S.). This is not to say that these effects will necessarily take place. The basis of our whole present society, though, will have to be reinterpreted in the light of a potential abundance of hardware and the widening gap between the affluent and the 'residual classes' (whether they be countries or people). The whole concept of working will have to be re-examined. Soon we may be paid a salary not to work, or given all those automatically produced luxuries as part of a 'social welfare' service, and this has been predicted to happen within the next ten years in the U.S. Perhaps the dole queue will be replaced by educational or 'self-help' centres, and people will be re-employed to learn.

The decision to continue in our present ways while developing embryonic cybernetically-controlled manufacturing processes is a political one and could lead to a great threat to 'internal security' as the dispossessed groups get larger. If, for instance, the present increase in unemployment and non-participation continues in the 'deprived areas' or 'economic ghettoes', the sense of despair, 'alienation' and demoralization could make itself felt in many political and violent ways. Thus by playing the 'World Economic Game' the 'social problems' within this country's society would grow. If, on the other hand, there is no automation, the threat of 'turmoil' or 'strife' is negligible. Perhaps with true British compromise, given the present situation, automation will continue only until a certain level of technological unemployment is reached, thus ensuring that the main cards for the battle of survival are kept in the hands of those in control. Maybe it's for this reason that Herman Kahn predicts that by the year 2,000, the U.K. will remain an early post-industrial society, while the rest of Europe and the U.S. will become 'visibly post-industrial'.

Education

The expenditure on education in this country, five per cent of the Gross National Product (more than twice as much as housing), is the direct result of what is partly assumption and partly shown by history, that better standards of living, production and economy occur through such spending. The power yielded by government through an education system is enormous; it can both restrict and encourage, support ambition and diminish hopes; by educational emphasis, it can specifically encourage those who are nationally and economically useful and restrict the passive to an unthinking, necessary, manual mass. Economic requirements produce a three-tier educational system: the first, the elite, are predominantly those from the middle or higher income groups and are channelled for the professions, business and government (of any they have a certain choice in life); the second are those trained to be skilled in some job, the great backbone of the country's industry (normally they are restricted to one trade, perhaps financially well-rewarded and controlled to the availability of work in predetermined areas). The third group are those left over, whose efforts are defined by work requirement with their economic gain varying immensely within pretty low limits. These people are usually academically less successful, tending to be part of passively uninterested communities, who have gained their apathy from poverty, bad education and bad housing.

24

The ever consuming vicious circle of poverty assures the 'cultural deprivation' of the 'dispossessed'. The multi-occupational, generally deteriorated, economic ghetto or slum, with its transient group movement, and its residual inhabitants, unskilled, unemployed, and uneducated, is the backdrop to education for the economically and socially 'alienated'. It is not uncommon for children to be illiterate or on probation for truancy. Mental illness, alcoholism and separation are their home comforts. Some parents are in prison. Maybe little or nothing can be done for, or with, the parents of children who face such serious problems in their homes. But these problems directly affect the children's health, attendance at school, emotional and personal adjustment. Their motor, linguistic and social behavioural patterns suffer, and in all probability some children will be school drop-outs.

It is 'economically determined' that the country needs a 'fluid mobile manual mass', who move to work as wanted and who are otherwise unemployed. The insecurity of inconsistent earnings, poor conditions and inability to change to more lucrative situations puts a social stress on the least fortunate of these people, which could be lessened by help through education. Self-identity and happiness could evolve from the sincere interest of and support by schools. The stability and individuality that the children's lives lack can be stimulated in the learning situation and maybe the school period is the only time when such sustained involvement is possible. However, the 'middle-class' ethic current in most schools, together with badly over-crowded conditions and badly overworked staff, do little to help schools fulfil their supporting role.

Traditional methods have been proved useless in slum areas, where the child's involvement is not merely with the conditioning of his mind, but with his physical survival, with the material gain he can obtain, although it is minimal, and with the overwhelming non-participatory, dream world of the entertainment media. These children are not less able; their surroundings represent a mental and physical poverty from which it is difficult to escape. If their education is looked at economically, the country is losing out on this part of the investment in ability. Since the school controls the most fruitful years of maturing, it could draw out confidence, support aims, point out possible lines of development and encourage initiative. A different approach and special attention to the education of poorer families have been established, but little work is being done to alleviate the original stress.

Basil Bernstein writes, in *New Society*, that seventy-nine per cent of secondary schools in slum areas are inadequate, as are their compensatory methods. Not only do they have overcrowded conditions to match those at home, but teacher turnover is high, and consistent individual interest lacking. When the adolescent leaves school, having learnt nothing that seems valid for his existence, and prepared only for the least demanding, least paid work, he is likely to become dependent on state aid. The apathy engendered by the senselessness and boredom at work, the lack of any direction and the impossibility of having any effect on his own situation contribute to this tendency. Perhaps the only subject likely to arouse community interest would be the improvement of his environment as a result of his own action. The school might indeed fire off such initiative but without substantial incentive and aid, financial and otherwise, apathy would remain.

Leisure

With the alleged 'leisure revolution' around the corner, who is going to enjoy the increasing time available, whether this be due to automation, shortening hours or unemployment? As the media have shown, their interest lies with those of 'middle-class aspirations' who partake, and not with those in the economic ghettoes who are unable to take part in the expanding 'industry' of leisure. The money needed is not available, unless some possible material gain is afforded. The leisure revolution bears no relevance to those in deprived areas. It is not tuned to them and only confirms their belief that they are outside society's norms, not able to obtain its gifts and afford its luxuries. The media encourage advertisements that suggest that the way to escape is 'Up, Up and Away'. Consumption of this sort depends on both greater income and more leisure.

The table shows that a semi-skilled person cannot afford to take time off. Pay is deducted. Holidays are less than two weeks long and the choice of when is limited. The unskilled man depends even more on daily work. Unlike the semi-skilled man, his opportunities for holidays are small if not non-existent. He cannot afford to go on holiday just as he cannot afford to stop

%	Semi-Skilled	Fore-men	White-Collar	Tech-nicians	Middle Managers	Senior Managers
holidays of 15+ days	38	72	74	77	84	88
choice of when	35	54	76	76	84	88
normal working 40+ hours	97	94	9	23	27	22
sick pay, employers' scheme	51	95	98	97	98	98
employers' pensions	67	94	90	94	96	96
time off for personal reasons	29	84	83	86	91	93
pay deductions for lateness	90	20	8	11	1	—
warning followed by dismissal for lateness	84	66	78	71	48	41
no clocking in or booking in	2	45	48	45	81	94

New Society

work. Usually those aspiring to the 'norms of society' will 'moonlight' (i.e. work at night) to better themselves. The wish to escape, though, is universal. Figures from the Institute of Community Studies urban report indicate that twenty-five per cent of 'middle income' families in Kensington had a second home, fifty-two per cent wanted one. Nobody had a second home in Hackney but sixty-six per cent wanted one. The increase in population has made space a precious commodity. The heavy population areas of the south-east mean that people have to travel much longer distances for leisure activities. The rise in transport rates and fares, and the rise in home prices, all seem to work against the deprived areas. As in the U.S., communities are becoming trapped in the urban environs. Children in them are only aware of a world of rotting houses and street surroundings. The nearest they get to partaking of any leisure is at the receiving end of a TV set, thus alienating them further. There is a trend away from 'place' communities to 'interest' communities, leaving the 'deprived' in a 'place' community, after everyone else has gone to an 'interest' community. Those in the upper socio-economic groups have increased mobility, both nationally and internationally, which allows them the luxury of 'dispersed-interest communities'. Social contacts and environmental mobility are now widening geographically, but it was found that whereas fifty-five per cent of upper income groups and thirty-five per cent of middle income groups had travelled more than 190 miles last year, only fourteen per cent of the lower income group did. Mobility is curtailed by the lack of cars and the high price of transport.

Leisure takes many forms, it is self-oriented or service-oriented, active or non-active, has physical or emotional involvements as a spectator or a participator, solitary or in company. If he is socially isolated because of increased distance between work stations, or the nature of his job, a man may tend towards sociable leisure activities. In urban areas these physical, active, participatory activities are inhibited by a lack of facilities, and so he is frustrated in this way. There is little education for leisure skills to compensate for non-involvement jobs or unemployment.

Authority and Media

As we have seen the 'protestant ethic' changed the whole way of life, completely redefining work and existence in a new context, repressing previous outlets and allowing for energies to be channelled elsewhere. Gradually with the increasingly complicated organization of life, man lost touch with previous simplicities; he became unable to cope with basic needs for security and could only accommodate these needs by providing larger organizations to deal with those problems previously dealt with by the community. The identity needed to replace these simple controls is gained, or half gained, by 'clan' membership so we see the rise of identity factions involved in nationalism and tribal affinities. It is this quest for identity, whether within the law or outside it, peaceful or violent, whether the symbol is a flower or a boot, discriminatory or all-embracing, that has affected a 'credibility gap', an alienation between the 'organizations' which now control our way of life. This anonymous authority encourages anonymity. It permeates down to cars, houses and even people. The all-encompassing anonymous authority depersonalizes and dehumanizes, before man is fed with his media fantasies. Through social control he learns what is expected of him, his social roles, the skills and motivations necessary for him to exist.

The bureaucratic hierarchical authority, what Faunce calls its rational-legal framework of multiple levels of supervision, its fixed official areas of action, an administration based on written documents and management through static rules, its 'non-volition' of responsibility and passive acceptance of roles in an area in which the worker has invested little of himself, not only 'alienates' its employees and the public, but demands the organizational behaviour of 'over-conformity', favouring an abdication of personal responsibilities and a 'I don't make the rules' attitude. Since independent human beings have no power, 'clan' membership is attained, usually mistakenly, in order to reinforce personal strength against bureaucracy.

As the 'organization' pressurizes its anonymity there occur minor 'rebellions' of small groups in search of a more meaningful identity. These groups 'personalize' themselves to guard against the greater impersonalization and to symbolize their grievances. They are seized upon by the media and popularized, so as to become a 'recognized cult form', rendering them manipulable by the establishment organizations, and becoming another condoned area of freedom. Invisible constraints affect our everyday life, giving the feeling of great freedom, but actually lessening it. Here the role of the media is to keep us happy and 'papped up'. It also acts as a reminder of the growing gap between those aspiring to the 'middle class' fantasies portrayed on the screens, and those in 'deprived' areas. The message coming across is almost, 'look, you *can't* have because you *can't* afford'. Any 'organization' will have to adapt these two roles of the media either towards 'potential revolution' or towards 'reinforcing existing internal security' depending on which side of the fence it sits. It may be that the inability to make frustration felt except by violence or taking to the streets, the total alienation from the larger and larger organizations, the lack of any affinities or identity with any 'condoned' dissent group, the total quashing of all hopes, aspirations and opportunities by 'the system', will give rise to a situation when, as Buckminster Fuller suggests, '. . . class warfare will force the invention of invisible architecture.' Who can attack the invisible? Who can rebel against nobody, or 'them' or 'it'? The mechanism for the survival of anonymous authority is 'conformity', a desire for acceptance by those aspiring to the 'controlled' images. People cannot accept themselves, because they are not themselves; we are conditioned commodities to be bought and sold and dealt with in an open market. If we are portrayed and propagandized and hence self-identified with a certain cultural and economic situation then we will play that given role; so that when we are told we are the 'underclass' we will behave in the way an 'underclass' is expected to behave. Pieces of paper represent people's rights and responsibilities. Pent-up frustration and unresolved social problems are dealt with by increasing the level and centralization of control. Apathy decreases alertness to infringements of civil liberties and 'conformity' reduces the likelihood that action will take place when the infringement is perceived.

'Residual Classes'

The 'working poor' were relatively successful in their struggle against exploitation. According to Harrington they accomplished something the 'capitalists' could never have done. A revolutionary situation came about not because of aggression by the capitalist overlords but through the achievements and efforts of the so-called 'exploited masses'. In the first stage of industrialization 'workers' fought for rights because they felt that they had literally nothing more to lose in the existing situation. They had scraped the barrel of human dignity; and though their protests, carried out in the name of revolution or 'total transformation', provoked partial reforms, the activists themselves gained a stake in, and consequently loyalty to, the capitalist society they opposed. As a result they moved from a visionary to a pragmatic ideology, though using the old capitalistic rules and often keeping the old language, even at the risk of 'alienating' their 'fellow workers'. In a recent Ford strike dispute, a union official (an aspirant to 'middle-class' values) said that the lessons that they had learnt from their failure were about communication (control points) causing the 'rank and file' to go against the decision of those representing them. The use of this term implies a breakdown in trust, apart from non-representation. The unskilled man is not only dispossessed in his economic, educational and leisure time environment by society as a whole, but also by its representatives, who are among those who 'made it'. So that any potential revolution tends to be led by a disenchanted middle class with guilt complexes, or those dispossessed who, with despair as their only security, have nothing to lose. The role of unions in the French and Italian 'revolts' are worth remembering in this context; their interests are more in terms of material and monetary rewards. The 'worker movement' has become so moderate as to be just a pressure group, seeking modifications on the distribution of G.N.P. without any desire to challenge the basic mechanism of ownership (witness the Liverpool G.E.C. takeover occupation bid). Buckminster Fuller sums it up:

World Society . . . has popularly misinterpreted higher productivity/hour and the concomitant requirement of lesser production hours/function in terms of social reform, as seemingly won by the only and hard way . . .

Industrial societies, especially in the west, for the first time in their history are not fundamentally challenged from within. There has been a modification of the old social war between the capitalist and worker; increasing affluence and white-collar service employees are the major factors in the subsidence of the war. This has meant that the middle income groups are supplying the values and aspirations for those in the lower socio-economic hierarchy, some of whom are accepting and aiming for these 'higher' goals. This group is divided into those affluent workers with non 'working-class' value systems, and those who have been 'left behind'. The war, if there is any, will not be between the 'working class' and the 'middle class' but between the 'residual class' and the rest of society. It will only happen if the aspirations and value systems of society are threatened by lack of security.

The group which is moving up the social scale does not behave in the same way as one which, tied to a 'working-class value system', considers itself fixed there for life. These aspirants have a sensitivity to the norms of the group they wish to move into. The unskilled man's potential for personal advancement is small. His security is limited and the greatest hope he has is for economic advancement, and that only within a union. 'Middle-class' prospects are seen in terms of ladder climbing. The 'middle class' tend to be more 'satisfied with their jobs', their leisure is seen as instrumental, and they belong more often to formal groups. In many respects the 'class' value systems are merging. Primary integration is more likely to be seen in terms of consumption patterns than basic values, which are usually linked to political attitudes or class loyalties. So the 'middle class' spreads to its aspirants with changes in occupational mobility and structure. They become the 'ex-poor' and the 'non-revolutionary proletariat', leaving behind the 'underclass', the 'residue'. Many people have written of the relationship between the 'disemployment' of physical workers and the increasing numbers of those in high technology work, inferring that the disemployed people tend to move into this field. But these are two separate parts of society, one the unskilled man with little education, the other from the intellectual elite, an entirely different socio-economic group.

As technical competence becomes the criterion for a position in the growing society, so some people are going to lose out, as they are already doing : then social tension is aroused. 'It is', as Eli Ginsberg suggests, 'the limits to "human capital" rather than financial capital which has become the fundamental element limiting the growth of society. It is not only the raising of "human capital" that is important but the problem of deciding what kind of "human capital".'

Let us now look at the possibilities for growth in a poverty area. Those unable to get out are frustrated by the so-called 'vicious circle of poverty', and live in bad conditions in an environment that has been decaying for many years. The children find their opportunities after their bad education very limiting, for without a good education they cannot get a good job, and without a good job they cannot afford the money for house renewals or moving out. The effect on the future generation is the same. The most certain thing about modern poverty is that it cannot be properly dealt with just by a relatively better distribution of income. The advance does not necessarily remove the specific frustrations of the environment. As we have seen, there is more than lack of money involved in 'poverty'.

In a simple matrix like this, we can see, in a general way, the mutual effects of various aspects of the environment on each other and on the whole.

Thus housing may depend on $1\frac{1}{2}$ factors (i.e. definitely employment and maybe social welfare), but $3\frac{1}{2}$ factors depend on housing

	Housing	Education	Leisure	Employment	Social Welfare	Food	
Housing		O	O	×	★	O	1½
Education	×		O	×	×	O	3
Leisure	★	×		×	★	O	3
Employment	★	×	O		×	O	2½
Social Welfare	×	★	O	×		★	3
Food	★	×	★	×	×		4
	3½	3½	½	5	4	½	Totals

O little effect (0)   ★ some effect (½)   × definite effect (1)

(definitely education and social welfare and maybe employment, leisure and food).

There is already a poor and insupportable group, albeit small in the U.K. though large in the U.S. ghettoes. The first task of survival is the satisfaction of human needs. Man's basic needs were summed up by Malinowski as being:

Human needs	Cultural responses
1. Metabolism	1. Commissarial
2. Reproduction	2. Kinship
3. Bodily comforts	3. Shelter
4. Safety	4. Protection
5. Movement	5. Activities
6. Growth	6. Training
7. Health	7. Hygiene

On a very superficial level we can see how 'culturally deprived' an area is.

According to Malinowski 'metabolism' represents the intake of energy and expulsion of waste material, not only in terms of human physiology but also as regards a community as a whole. Every organism requires certain conditions which assure a supply of physical material to enable it to live. The cultural response to the particular needs imposed by 'metabolism' consists of a set of institutions. The actual make-up of the family means that the main area of food intake and consumption activity is within this group. Where nutrition depends on the effective working of a whole chain of preparatory activities and linked institutions, anything affecting the chain anywhere would also affect basic satisfactions. Thus a whole series of conditions become necessary and indispensable to the biological performance of placing food into someone's mouth. And yet within 'deprived' areas many children are fed only at schools as they cannot rely upon being fed at home. The links in the chain of activities are, in fact, so imperfect as to render the whole process useless. They exist in that a man goes to work to get money, to pay for shelter, clothing and food. But it is 'deprivation' when a child cannot eat at home because of an environmental/economic situation outside the control of the individual family, or the parents rely on 'vitamin-enriched' pet food for protein because they have no work or do not get enough assistance from the state due to poor functioning of various institutions. It is believed that two million families in Britain are living on or below the poverty line.

'Reproduction' can be seen not only in terms of individual sex, but in terms of the life or death of a community. The act is linked up with the fact of legally founded parenthood, a relationship in which the parents, or an extended family, look after the children for a long period of time. Traditional reinterpretations which draw in physiological factors, influences from the environment and from the interaction of the other members of the community, have changed the natural parental instincts into 'highly removed bonds of social solidarity'. Not only is this social solidarity non-existent in 'deprived' areas but the father/mother relationship tends to be under more stress than in areas of better environments. Many families have only one parent and these, as has been shown by the Child Poverty Action Group, are some of the more critical poor. Mental illness, crime and divorce rates also show a larger percentage break-up of families in economic ghettoes. Many women have to work (even on a part-time basis) to keep the family, and this means they have no alternative but to leave their child unattended or to hire 'nannies' (which is economically crippling). The nurseries that exist are very scattered and overcrowded, as are primary and secondary schools, but it is when there is nobody available to guide and look after the child, or no school that can accept him because of the already massive problems of overcrowding, that the mother/father solidarity starts to break. In December 1969 over 7,000 children in Britain were in the care of the local authorities as a result of family breakdown. It is in these areas that communities do not exist. 'Non-communities' exist where inhabitants are transient and only a small percentage are unable to get out. 'Bodily comforts' reflect metabolic reactions to the natural elements. Clothing, warmth, shelter, the equipment to wash are necessary. Human beings do not look for shelter in a haphazard way, but because of deprivation are forced to live in houses unfit for human habitation, where many rooms are unliveable in. Often there is no money for heat; clothing is worn continuously day and night. There is probably an outside W.C., but no hot water and no bath. One must remember the context in which we are speaking. It is a highly industrialized nation in 1970 which signed the 1948 United Nations resolution on housing standards. Eleven per cent of the housing stock in Britain is in a sub-standard category.

'Safety' is prevention from injuries. When most organisms are not protected from injury the culture and its group will die. Organization against danger involves such 'institutions' as the household and the community. Protection means being able to see the consequences of certain actions on the organism in terms of planning, construction and maintenance of buildings. 'Here the economic factor in the organized, technically planned and co-operatively executed principles of selection, construction and maintenance enters clearly and definitely'. Many houses in 'deprived' areas are damp, structurally unsound, hence dangerous to health and life. The landlord (public or private) refuses to repair because of pressures of demand. If they are 'blighted' why bother with improvements? Yet, because of the shortage of housing, people have no alternative but to pay rent. Many families will not claim rebates for fear of being discriminated against on government housing lists. Often the security of a 'community' is absent in this situation and there is no group redress.

'Movement' is an activity necessary to an organism or community and indispensable to 'culture'. It involves the general conditions in which a group of people live and co-operate and under which most people at any one time and everyone at some time or another has obtained some scope for exercise and initiative. The system of bodily activities connected with economic life, political organizations, exploration of the environment and contact with other communities is related to individual muscle tensions and the surplus of nervous energy. Play and recreation are seen in terms of their educational value and their function as a preparation for skills needed in the outside economic environment. Most play and recreation facilities are non-existent within the 'alienated' part of society, except for the streets. Education and leisure activities, as has been previously seen, offer no help to break the circle of poverty. People who had initiative or any mobility orientation have moved out; those left are the 'dispossessed'. The 'non-community' does not exist as a co-operating entity. Those falling back on 'normlessness' in politico-economic activities do so out of a sense of total despair, while the 'powerlessness' and 'deprivation' of their cultural environment render many of them totally apathetic.

'Growth' is maturation, a gradual process imposing certain general but very definite conditions on culture. Education and training synthesizes all past and projected cultural experiences, enabling an individual to combat exterior pressures in his personal environment. It is the manner in which a person is taught some necessary skills and the use of a language and initiated into the ever widening set of institutions of which he will become a full member. As has been shown, the inequality of the 'equality of education' ensures that the institutions open to an individual from a 'depressed area' are numbered and that he will never even become a full member of 'society'. In London an average of sixty per cent of adolescents stayed beyond the minimum leaving age; in Hackney sixty-six per cent leave school at fifteen. Early leaving ensures a bad job which ensures a bad house which is part of a bad environment. The early leaver could be a 'no-chance' person.

'The maintenance of an organism or community in normal conditions as regards its capacity for an indispensable output of energy,' is health. 'Hygiene' is the cultural response to the health of a community. Bad sanitary conditions, with no hot water or bath and an outside toilet, have been discussed above. Even at this brief glance we can see that basic cultural responses are not fulfilled in these areas. The economic ghettoes contain both black and white, in fact, according to the Race Relations Board there are no racial ghettoes in London ; the highest percentage of immigrants in one ward being thirty per cent, and in a borough – eighteen per cent. The Child Poverty Action Group has recently brought out a report, which mentions five sorts of people living in poverty. These are the old, the disabled, the fatherless families, the long-term unemployed and the 'poverty' wage earners. One in six earn less than £17 average weekly wage. Over one-fifth of the population now rely wholly or partly on state aid, as against $2\frac{3}{4}$ million a few years ago. Meanwhile average earnings for the male worker have increased fifty-four per cent and weekly national insurance benefits have gone up forty-eight per cent in the period from May 1963 to October 1969. The average earnings of the lowest ten per cent of male manual workers has gone down from the 1960 value of seventy-one per cent of the national average weekly wage to sixty-seven per cent in 1968. Low-income families have not been given priority and in some respects they have even lost ground. *New Society* summed up the situation by saying that there was an

. . . increasing isolation of a relatively poor, but still more, a 'deprived' minority at the bottom end of the spectrum. Even if this group enjoys a guaranteed minimum income, or benefits from negative income tax, it is likely to be under-educated, under-skilled and relatively unemployable. It is certainly going to be increasingly envious of the great majority enjoying education, skills, secure and interesting jobs. It may be just sullen and apathetic, it may turn to violence. It will certainly display wildly above average indices of mental disturbance, family break-up and petty disturbance of the social order. It will place disproportionate demands on welfare and remedial service. It is almost without doubt THE urban problem of the 1990's.

Behaviour

The shifting of people under ecological pressures brings about an association of 'like with like' and a tendency for population 'specialization' in certain areas. The social area has little geographical frame of reference for the middle class. Friends are at the other end of a telephone, miles away, but those in 'deprived' areas have no phones. Their friends, if any, are around them, the social area has a geographical meaning and contains people having the same level of living and way of life. Fares are expensive and few people have cars, so they cannot get out. In theory people can escape from their surroundings, but in practice the culture of poverty induces a sense of despair of ever being able to escape. Social institutions and transmitted value systems can create a sense of confinement no less demoralizing than a prison.

The ecological concentrations of certain forms of mental illness follow the pattern of social groupings especially in those parts of a large city which are overcrowded and where there is social disorganization. Many studies confirmed findings that alcoholism, family break-up, suicide, delinquency and numerous other forms of 'disturbed behaviour' are most prevalent in 'deprived areas'. In one study it was found that those lowest in the socio-economic scale in this country had over forty-five per cent of the schizophrenia cases. Whereas suicide is largely due to social isolation, attempted suicide has been found to be highly correlated with overcrowded conditions, friction within a domestic group largely due to cramped premises, the instability of parental 'solidarity' and the difficulty of forming stable relationships.

Within these areas the stimulus to develop impossible expectations and fantasies seems to come from a sense of inner insecurity, hopelessness and total loss of confidence in individual fate. Aspirations are, according to H. Argyle, the self-goal-giving, continually readjustable non-satisfactions of existing desires, fantasies and escapades. They are the results of our respective conditionings within and without the family context. Economic and political activities are among the influences that lead to the raising of value aspirations. When these aspirations are raised and no satisfaction outlets exist, frustration is built up. The 'J-curve' theory of socio-economic development suggests that when aspirations are raised by government influences in the economy, but actual improvement does not meet the level of these continually rising aspirations, the gap between the aspirations and the actual rise in the standard of living widens. It is when the gap reaches a certain magnitude that 'relative deprivation' sets in where there are no facilities to release the energies caused by the increase of frustrations. What has probably happened in Britain is that sudden improvements in social circumstances gave rise to hopes of better things to come. The actual improvement was not sufficiently high to meet newly aroused expectations, and an 'intolerable' gap between expectation and attainment ensued, constituting 'systematic frustration'. One of the facets of our economic system is the need for continual consumption, to the eventual end that every desire must be satisfied immediately and no wish must be denied. The media encourage this, industry makes it possible with hire-purchase and instalment plans. Yet if these external conditions change and things do not fit any more into familiar social and economic characteristics, a lag arises, which often changes the functions of these characteristics into an element of disintegration instead of stabilization.

In an economically and socially stable situation, people tend to consolidate their position in 'society' by aspiring to limited but obtainable goals. In unstable conditions these limits tend to disappear and a whole spectrum of practical and impractical desires is released in the ensuing insecurity, making it difficult to restrain these aspirations. As 'wants' are always based on keeping up with the aspirational gap between the 'haves' and 'have-nots' in the socio-economic hierarchy, these insecurities can be exacerbated and can lead to mental and physical pressures. Erich Fromm in his book, *The Sane Society*, suggests that the mental task which man must set himself is not to feel secure but to be able to tolerate his insecurity. If these insecurities get too much for him to cope with, he may change his attitude about getting rid of them legally. We are often under great pressure to be successful within the system, though not so much stress is put on how we gain this success, and since there is basically unequal access to success, such as through economic security, those who do not make it can end up using illegal methods. So the less access to legitimate channels of socio-economic progress, the greater the build-up of frustrations, the greater 'deviant behaviour' such as violence, and the greater build-up of social pressures in poor and 'deprived' areas.

As with aspirations, the structure of society and the function of the individual in the social framework determine the content of social character. The necessity to unite, and relate with other things or human beings, is thwarted many times in the 'economic ghettoes' and 'deprived areas' of industrial cities. The problems resulting from this are expanding rapidly. Mental health disorders are affecting more and more people in these communities. Many problems become neuroses. In this case some people may be unable to hold a job continuously and there is a total breakdown in a person's self-relationship; he can no longer cope without help. If, as is usually the case, there is no help forthcoming he can become more 'mentally disturbed'. Schizophrenia involves a withdrawal from 'persistent volitional behaviour'. Manic depression with its accompanying judgement disturbances, paranoia involving delusions of grandeur and persecution, and anxiety states, phobias and obsessions are all far more common than in 'affluent' areas. There are various social reasons for these anxiety neuroses. Schizophrenics tend to be isolated both socially and within the family, conflicting with both the content and manner of communication. Paranoia also occurs with isolated people, people not able to test their beliefs with others because of poor social contacts. Manic depression is often found in deprived areas where the whole family is involved in a situation of failure; failure to progress, failure to break out and above all acknowledgement of failure of 'self'. Pseudo-social delinquency, which is characterized by different behaviour between friends, and towards people outside the group, including an attitude of hostility to authority, finds its origins within the 'deprived areas', in the neglected homes and the rejection of social mores; the group usually rejects society. It can be seen that the areas of highest 'delinquency' are the twilight zones, where there is little family life, no community facilities or amenities, and where residential buildings mingle with commercial, industrial plots. In one study it was found that seventy-three per cent of 'juvenile delinquents' originated from overcrowded conditions and fifty per cent came from broken homes or a disturbed parental situation.

The purpose of this rather generalized look at the problems affecting the lives of many people trapped in the inner urban cores has been to paint a picture of the setting in which the surveys were taken, and the conclusions made. In this battle for survival of the fittest it has been shown overall how the cards are stacked against a specific group of people. It is as if the situation between the rich and poor nations of the world has been mirrored and telescoped to micro-level; the same exploitation and domination games are still played with equal ruthlessness. Let us now examine this micro-level.

4. Economic Survey

The area between Hornsey Rise and Archway Road is a 'deprived' area. It does not fulfil cultural responses to basic needs. Its houses are in a state of decay due both to landlord and G.L.C. neglect, and also to the proposed redevelopment that was first put forward six years ago and is not likely to be brought to fruition for several years to come.

The houses suffer from rising damp, woodworm and dry rot. In many cases windows remain broken for years mainly because the landlord, whether private or public, does not consider it worthwhile to repair them. Most houses have an outside toilet, no bath and no hot water. Some housing is the responsibility of the welfare department which houses those evicted people who have nowhere else to go. It is impossible for many of these people to be rehoused in council flats until they pay off their rent arrears which they often cannot do. Many times the children's department will pay the rent in order not to split up the family. Many families will exist on social security payments; a family of six will get approximately £19 per week, whereas if the father worked he would only bring in £14.

The majority of people living there are unskilled manual workers; many have been unemployed for long periods of time. Educationally, this is a priority area. The schools need money, teachers and facilities. When the children leave school their choice of jobs is very limited; some may be fortunate enough to get into public service industries thus providing, for the first time, a form of security. Those with initiative get out of the area. Most have no alternative but to take any available work. There are seasonal and government changes in unemployment that hit areas like this one much harder than anywhere else.

This instability leads to great pressures on family and home life. A large percentage of emotionally disturbed and mentally ill people live in these areas. There are more social workers, health and social welfare clinics than in non-deprived areas. The N16 area to the east of Hornsey Rise (from where many people in this area come) is a very similar area. It had 113 per cent of the national rate of psychiatric patient discharges in 1969; this is an increase of 28 per cent over the 1965–7 period. During this period the increase was 49 per cent in Hackney. Admissions had gone up 17 per cent and, in Hackney, schizophrenia admissions were 154 per cent of the national average.

Play and leisure facilities are non-existent and, excepting the streets and the betting shops, there is only T.V. Very few families have cars, even fewer have telephones. They are, according to the police, not even very good criminals. They are trapped in a vicious circle of poverty, they cannot get out of these economic ghettoes. They are the 'no-chance' people.

To understand the situation in this area fully, a survey was taken to validate the widening gap between those aspiring to middle-class values and those left behind. The survey took the form of two questionnaires, the first dealing with employment and housing, and the second dealing with social alienation. The purpose of the economic survey was to see if a group of people existed who were identifiably worse off than the majority of the others, and to isolate them. Having shown that they were economically alienated, they were followed up for social isolation and alienation. Many proved not to be sociologically alienated but a substantial percentage were found to be alienated both economically and socially, and this group has grown within the last five years.

Survey

For the first survey a run-down sample was taken of forty-eight households within the area of:

Mulkern Road	Duncombe Road
Nicolay Road	Calverley Grove
Sussex Way	St Johns Way

The average age of those interviewed was mid-thirties.

For the second survey, most of the people were followed up; due to time factors involved only thirty-five were interviewed. Also interviewed were a group of homeless families in Hillside welfare hotel. These were in:

Mulkern Road   St Johns Way
Nicolay Road   Duncombe Road
Sussex Way

These are the questions asked in the first survey:

1. How long have you been living here?
2. Where did you live before?
3. Why did you leave?
4. Is this a better place?
5. How many people live here?
6. How many rooms have you?
7. Who owns this place?
8. Who owned your last place?
9. How much rent do you pay?
10. How much rent did you pay at your last place?
11. Are you getting state help (social security supplementary benefit, family allowance, rent)?
12. Do you work — if so what?
13. Does your husband work — if so what?
14. How much are you getting at your job ($<£10$, $<£13$, $<£15$, $<£17$, $<£20$, $>£20$)
15. How much were you getting at your job five years ago?
16. How many times in the last five years have you been unemployed (and job changes)?
17. How many times in the last year have you been unemployed?
18. Do you find it more difficult to find a job now than five years ago?
19. Do you find it more difficult to make ends meet than five years ago?
20. Remarks.

It was found that **45% IN THE AREA HAD BEEN IN THEIR PRESENT HOUSES**

				for 5 years and less
21%	,,	,,	,,	between 5 and 10 years
2%	,,	,,	,,	between 10 and 15 years
32%	,,	,,	,,	over 20 years

The area is made up of two major blocks of people; those who have been there five years or less and those who have been there

32% of households > 20 yrs
2% < 15 yrs
21% < 10 yrs
45% < 5 yrs

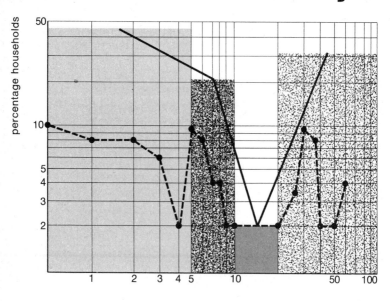

percentage households

50

10

5
4
3

2

1   2   3 4 5   10   50   100

years

of those there less than 5 years
23%	6 mnths
18%	6 mnths to 1 yr
18%	1 yr to 2 yrs
14%	2 yrs to 3 yrs
23%	4 yrs to 5 yrs

over twenty years. Two facts account for this: the transience of the population made up of unskilled manual workers, and the proposed redevelopment of the area. This area is used by many people as a staging post. They come to this area out of desperation. There is nowhere else to go. This can be seen by the fact that 66 per cent of those who moved into this area to get more room moved to premises that had no hot water, no bath, and an outside toilet. The area is adjacent to the East End enclave. It relies on local and suburban industry as a hinterland, although these are not flourishing.

The redevelopment of the area was proposed six years ago. Since then the G.L.C. has been very slowly buying up houses. Many of these have been left to decay, although some continue to be used by the G.L.C., by the housing welfare department and housing associations because housing pressures in Islington are so great.

The effect of this can be seen in the second table where of the 45 per cent who have been living in the area for the last five years:

23%	HAD BEEN THERE		LESS THAN 6 MONTHS
18%	,,	,,	,, 5 months–1 year
18%	,,	,,	,, 1–2 years
14%	,,	,,	,, 2–3 years
4%	,,	,,	,, 3–4 years
23%	,,	,,	,, 4–5 years

Of those 21% who had been living there for between 5–10 years:

40%	HAD BEEN THERE		LESS THAN 6 YEARS
20%	,,	,,	,, 6–7 years
20%	,,	,,	,, 7–8 years
10%	,,	,,	,, 8–9 years
10%	,,	,,	,, 9–10 years

What is also shown in the logarithmic graph are the three waves of migration into the area; the first thirty to thirty-five years ago just after the depression, the second five to ten years ago during the 'never had it so good' period, and finally during the last three years. This was due mostly to government housing activity and its positive and negative results.

66% of those moving for more room in last 5 years moved to places that had outside w.c., no bath, no hot water

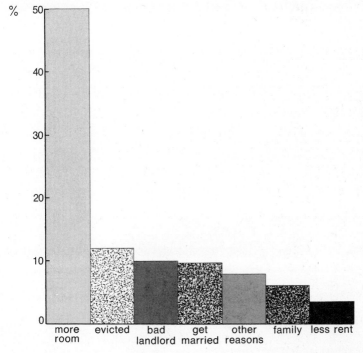

% 50

40

30

20

10

0

more room | evicted | bad landlord | get married | other reasons | family | less rent

reasons to move

Those living in the area over twenty years are a significant group; 32 per cent of the survey had been living there for this length of time. Reasons include a lack of initiative to get out as the place decayed because work and housing possibilities are insecure, and rents are low.

8%	WERE BORN IN THIS AREA
50%	COME FROM WITHIN 1 MILE RADIUS
23%	,, ,, ,, 1–3 MILES RADIUS
13%	,, ,, ,, 3–5 MILES RADIUS
2%	,, ,, ,, OVER 5 MILES IN LONDON
4%	,, ,, ,, OUTSIDE LONDON

The conditions people were living in were decaying. Many made do with overcrowded circumstances. Many had neither bath, hot water nor an inside toilet, and were living in buildings that were damp and structurally damaged. Yet what made people move into this area?

50%	SAID THE REASONS WERE MORE ROOM
12%	,, ,, ,, ,, EVICTIONS
10%	,, ,, ,, ,, BAD LANDLORDS
10%	,, ,, ,, ,, GETTING MARRIED
8%	,, ,, ,, ,, OTHER REASONS
6%	,, ,, ,, ,, FAMILY REASONS
4%	,, ,, ,, ,, LESS RENT

Some people gave more than one reason.

Of the 50 per cent who had moved for more room half of these had been there less than five years although nearly all moved into worse conditions. 66 per cent of those who moved for more room within the last five years moved to places that had an outside toilet, no bath and no hot water, purely because the housing situation is tight. This was due mostly to pressure on family space; some were prepared to put up with these conditions in the hope that when the G.L.C. bought up their houses they would be rehoused. Nearly a quarter of the sample were thrown out of their previous flat or house, or had bad landlord experiences. Of those evicted 100 per cent had been in the area less than five years and 75 per cent of those who left because of landlord trouble were also newcomers to the area. As can be expected 50 per cent of those who moved to get married and set up house had been there over ten years.

8% born here
50 from 1 mile radius
23   1·3
13   3·5
2   over 5
4   outside LONDON

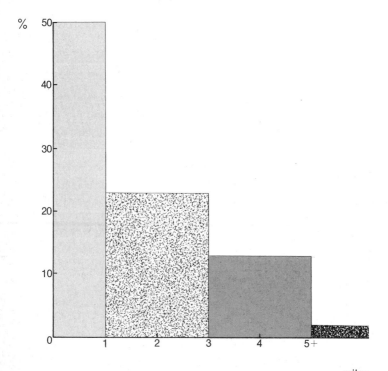

miles

Of those interviewed:

33% FOUND THEIR PRESENT PLACE BETTER; OF THESE 55% HAD BEEN THERE LESS THAN 5 YEARS (18% of total)

55% „ „ „ „ WORSE, „ 50% HAD BEEN THERE LESS THAN 5 YEARS (27% of total)

6% „ „ „ „ BETTER ORIGINALLY BUT NOW VERY DETERIORATED

6% HAD NOTHING TO JUDGE BY, AS THEY HAD BEEN THERE ALL THEIR LIFE.

Of those who found their present place better:

60% OF THE TOTAL HAD NO OUTSIDE TOILET
60% „ „ „ „ „ BATH
40% „ „ „ „ „ HOT WATER

The relationship between bad sanitary conditions and length of time in the area:

OF THOSE WHO HAD BEEN THERE 5 YEARS OR LESS 50% HAD NO INSIDE W.C.
45% „ „ BATH
22% „ „ HOT WATER
OF THOSE WHO HAD BEEN THERE BETWEEN 5–20 YEARS 63% HAD NO INSIDE W.C.
63% „ „ BATH
27% „ „ HOT WATER
OF THOSE WHO HAD BEEN THERE OVER 20 YEARS 37% HAD NO INSIDE W.C.
80% „ „ BATH
80% „ „ HOT WATER

It can be seen that those who have been living in the area for over twenty years are far worse off in regard to basic hygienic requirements.

no

.... in. w.c.
___ hot water
_ _ bath

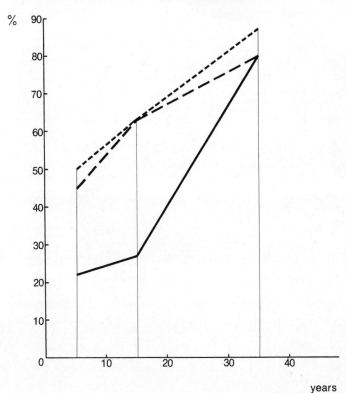

The average density for this area is 1·05 persons per usable room. It was decided to consider the usable rooms as a unit, because it was found during the survey that most houses had one or two rooms that were not usable due to damp or wood-worm and that this would give a more realistic picture of the situation.

length of stay in area	number of people	number of usable rooms	total number of rooms	average p/ur	average p/r
5 years or less	122	103	116	1·2	1·05
5–20 years	65	69	72	0·95	0·9
more than 20 years	70	72	84	0·975	0·83
TOTAL	257	244	272	1·05	0·95

Forty-eight per cent of the people living in this area have lived here for five years or less at a density of 1·2 persons/usable room. Those who moved in the last five years for more room are living at a density of 1·3 persons/usable room. Forty-five per cent of these were living at a density greater than 1·5 persons/usable room and eighteen per cent of these were living at a density greater than 2·0 persons/usable room.

At the present time 48% OF HOUSES ARE OWNED BY PRIVATE LANDLORD OR AGENCY
39% ,,   ,,   ,,   ,,   ,, HOUSING ASSOCIATION HAVING OBTAINED THEM FROM THE COUNCIL
37% ,,   ,,   ,,   ,,   ,, THE COUNCIL AND THE G.L.C.
4% ,,   ,,   ,, OWNER OCCUPIED
2% OF THE HOUSES GO WITH THE JOB

Of those who had been there less than five years, forty-two per cent were in council houses (all of which had been private before being bought by the G.L.C.); they had moved away from private landlords, mostly to private dwellings which were later relinquished to the council. Only ten per cent had previously been in council housing.

THOSE WHO MOVED FOR MORE ROOM LIVE AT A DENSITY OF 1·3 p/ur
of these 45% > 1·5 p/ur
18% > 2·0 p/ur

housing distribution

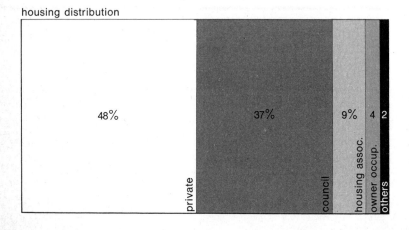

48%

37%

9%

4

2

private

council

housing assoc.

owner occup.

others

RENT

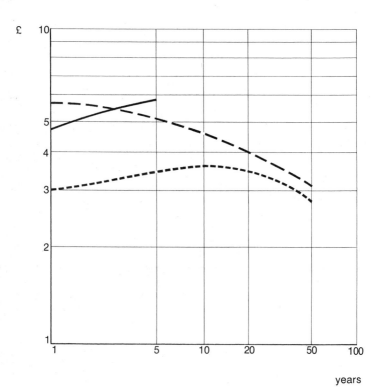

USABLE ROOMS

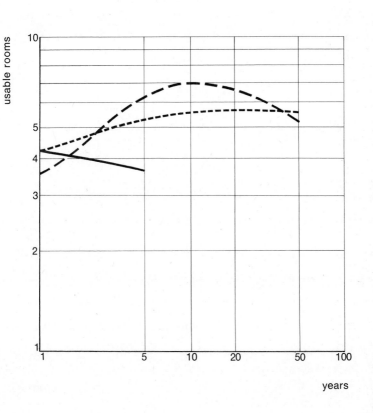

years

families < level of subsistence

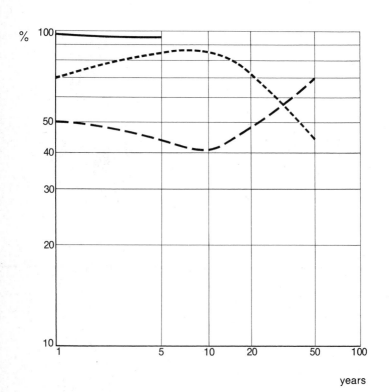

years

households < N.A.W.

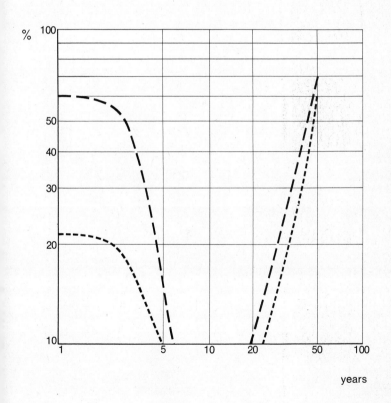

years

G.L.C. Average council housing situation

	rent	number of usable rooms	number of people	total income into households	previous rent	previous income
5 years or less	£3	4·3	6	£22.2	£3.13.8	£15
5–20 years	£3.13	5·6	5·6	£21.5	£6.18	£19
Over	£2.17	5·6	4·3	£16.15	—	£16.6

Average private housing situation

5 years or less	£5.7	3·6	4·2	£20	£3.11	£13.14
5–20 years	£4.11	7	10·6	£25	£3.3	£21
Over 20 years	£3.3	5·2	4·3	£16.13	—	£16

Average rent of white and black people in private landlord's flat

BLACK	£6.10	2·3	4	£18	£5.7.6	£13
WHITE	£4.13	4·4	4·6	£21	£2.9	£14.2

Average housing association situation. All have been there five years or less :

	£5.6	4·3	5·6	£19.10	£7.12.6	£17.10

Among those who are in G.L.C. tenancy and who have been here five years or less :

> 30% ARE UNSKILLED MANUAL WORKERS
> 30% ARE SKILLED
> 10% ARE SEMI-SKILLED
> 10% ARE WHITE COLLAR

Within the private landlord sector thirty-eight per cent of those who moved within the last five years are black. It can be noticed that blacks pay over thirty per cent more for approximately half the rooms that the whites get. Mind you, five years ago they were paying fifty per cent more.

JOB DISTRIBUTION

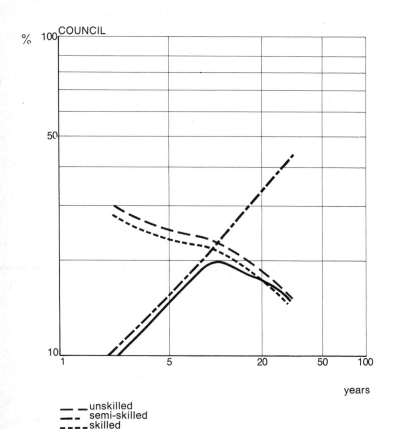

COUNCIL

%   100

50

10

1   5   20   50   100

years

- - unskilled
-- - semi-skilled
--- skilled
—— white-collar

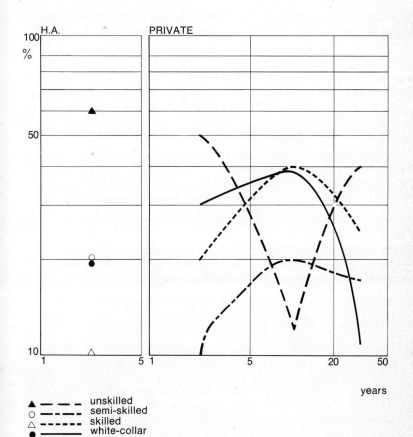

H.A.

PRIVATE

years

▲ — — — unskilled
○ — · — · — semi-skilled
△ · · · · · · skilled
● ———— white-collar

It can be seen that those housed by the housing associations are paying the same rent on average as those in private tenancy who have been there less than five years, and up to forty per cent more than those housed by G.L.C. and private sectors. Of these

60% ARE UNSKILLED MANUAL WORKERS
20% ARE SEMI-SKILLED
20% ARE WHITE COLLAR

Twenty-two per cent of households have incomes that are even less than National Average Wage (N.A.W.). These people are living at about one person per usable room (p/ur) density, but are paying only seventy-eight per cent of the average rent. Of these fifty per cent are living at a density of over 2·5 p/ur. But whereas their average income has risen fifteen per cent (the national cost-of-living index has increased fifty per cent) in the last five years, those who are earning N.A.W. level or above have seen their income rise over thirty per cent. Thus, those house-holds which have incomes less than N.A.W. are far worse off now in relation to those whose income is above N.A.W. Seventy-seven per cent of households are below the poverty line.

Among those who are in private accommodation and who have been there five years or less:

50% ARE UNSKILLED MANUAL WORKERS
20% ARE SKILLED
30% ARE WHITE COLLAR

As can be noticed there are no semi-skilled workers in this group. In a larger survey the category of semi-skilled workers would also be negligibly represented in this group.

Sixty-three per cent of households are earning below N.A.W. and living at a density of 1·3 p/ur and pay twelve per cent more than the average rent. One of the reasons seems to be that of this sixty-three per cent some forty per cent are black (twenty-five per cent of the total group). Of this sixty-three per cent, sixty per cent are living at over 1·5 p/ur density of which twenty per cent are black (twelve per cent of the total group). But whereas their average income has risen twelve per cent (blacks forty-four per cent) over the last five years, those households earning more than N.A.W. income level saw their income rise thirty-three per cent (of this group thirty per cent are black).

Although on average this group's average wage has increased thirty-one per cent, the income of the black people has only gone up twenty-seven per cent. Half of these families were existing at a level below government subsistence recommendation.

Fifty per cent of the households in the housing association group are earning less than N.A.W. and living at 1·7 p/ur. Of the total group fifty per cent are black, and it is in this group that earnings have either remained static or actually gone down by as much as eighteen per cent. The total average income has increased by ten per cent in the last five years. Meanwhile those households which are earning more than N.A.W. have seen their income rise twenty-three per cent. All families were living below the level of subsistence.

No families are earning an income less than N.A.W. in either the private or public sectors of housing among those who have lived in the area between five and twenty years, although nearly one hundred per cent of those in houses now controlled by the council or G.L.C. and forty per cent of those in private housing were living below government subsistence level of £5 per person per week.

Of those who have been in the area over twenty years and are now housed by the G.L.C. (their houses had been bought by the council while they were still in them) :

15% ARE UNSKILLED MANUAL WORKERS
43% ARE SEMI-SKILLED
14% ARE SKILLED
14% ARE WHITE COLLAR
14% HAVE PENSIONS

Fifty per cent of the households are earning less than N.A.W. and living at a density of 0·75 p/ur.

The unskilled manual workers are living at the highest density of the group at one p/ur; their average income has not risen during the last five years, but has remained static. (This is shown in the national cost-of-living index as a relative decline.) Those earning less than N.A.W. have seen their income remain static or decline very slightly, and those earning more than N.A.W. have only increased their income by one per cent over the last five years. Fifty per cent of households were below the poverty line.

Among those in the private sector:

42% ARE UNSKILLED MANUAL WORKERS
17% ARE SEMI-SKILLED
25% ARE SKILLED
 9% ARE WHITE COLLAR
 7% HAVE A PENSION

Forty-five per cent of households who have been in the area longer than twenty years have an income level less than N.A.W. and are living at a density of 0·88 p/ur, but a quarter of this group are living at more than two persons per usable room.

The income of those households who rely on unskilled manual workers has dropped by over one per cent over the last five years. Those households earning more than N.A.W. have had their incomes raised by 1·2 per cent; but sixty-six per cent of households in the private sector are living below government subsistence level.

So it can be seen that those in the worst economic situation are the unskilled manual workers who have been in the area less than five years or more than twenty years and especially those in private accommodation. Thirty per cent of all households were earning less than N.A.W. (i.e. £17) at an average of £13.30. Of these fifty per cent had been living in their place less than five years and fifty per cent over twenty years.

% JOB CHANGE OR UNEMPLOYED
in last 5 years

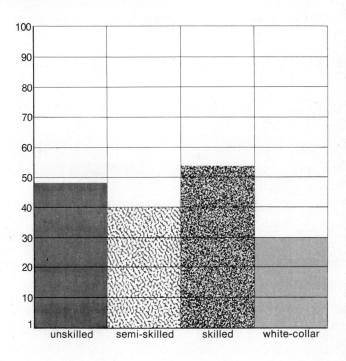

% JOB CHANGE
in last 5 years

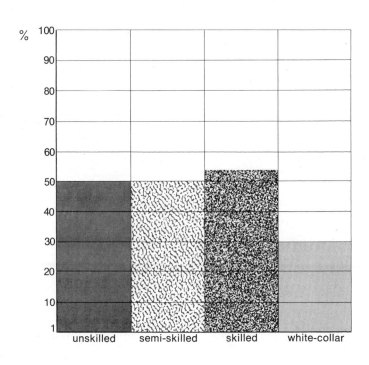

% **JOB CHANGE last year**

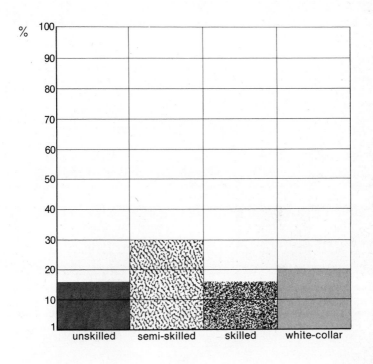

% UNEMPLOYMENT
in last 5 years

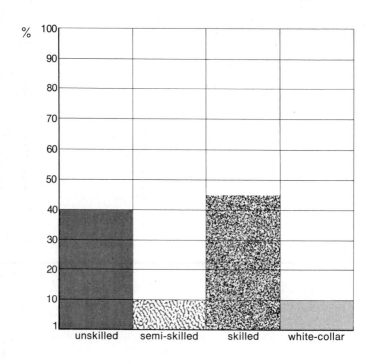

% UNEMPLOYED
last year

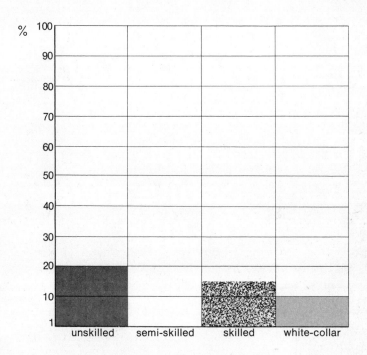

**OF THOSE EARNING
LESS THAN N.A.W.**
60% are unskilled
18   semi
 8   white collar
14   skilled

Workforce and Employment

	Un-skilled	Skilled	Semi-skilled	White Collar	
% workforce who changed jobs or were unemployed in last 5 years	48	54	40	30	%
Average length of unemployment per unemployed person in last year	3	$3\frac{1}{2}$	0	1	weeks
Average length of unemployment per unemployed person in last 5 years	2	2	$4\frac{1}{2}$	0·14	weeks/ years
Average rate of unemployment in last year	1	1	0	1	times/ year
Average rate of unemployment in last 5 years	0·3	0·5	0·2	0·2	times/ year
Average number of job changes for those who changed jobs in last year	2	1	1	1	
Average number of job changes for those who changed jobs in last 5 years	2·5	4	$2\frac{1}{4}$	$2\frac{2}{3}$	
% workforce unemployed in last year	20	15	0	10	%
% workforce unemployed in last 5 years	40	45	10	10	%
% workforce who changed jobs in last year	16	16	30	20	%
% workforce who changed jobs in last 5 years	50	54	50	30	%

It can be seen that the unskilled and skilled are the most threatened categories of workers, as has been shown in the previous report. With automation and economic pressures increasing these two groups of workers will find increasing hardship; the unskilled because they have neither the training nor the opportunities, and the skilled because they tend to be too specialized. Thus there were a greater proportion of skilled and unskilled workers who changed jobs or were unemployed in the last five years. Their average length of unemployment was greater by over a third in the last year. The rate of unemployment for skilled workers both during last year and in the last five years was slightly higher than the rate for semi-skilled and unskilled workers.

This breakdown, however, does not show where the real hardship lies except that it points to the unskilled and skilled workers. A further breakdown which pinpointed the economically alienated groups, by surveying those workers earning less than N.A.W. and studying their make-up, was made.

Having dealt with the workforce as a whole, a further breakdown was necessary to determine those in great difficulty.

Of the workforce earning less than N.A.W.:

> 60% ARE UNSKILLED MANUAL WORKERS
> 14% ARE SEMI-SKILLED
> 18% ARE SKILLED
> 8% ARE WHITE COLLAR

50% OF THESE UNSKILLED MANUAL WORKERS HAVE CHANGED THEIR JOBS OR WERE UNEMPLOYED OVER THE LAST 5 YEARS

25% OF THESE SEMI-SKILLED MANUAL WORKERS HAVE CHANGED THEIR JOBS OR WERE UNEMPLOYED OVER THE LAST 5 YEARS

30% OF THESE SKILLED MANUAL WORKERS HAVE CHANGED THEIR JOBS OR WERE UNEMPLOYED OVER THE LAST 5 YEARS

30% OF THESE WHITE-COLLAR WORKERS HAVE CHANGED THEIR JOBS OR WERE UNEMPLOYED OVER THE LAST 5 YEARS

26% OF THESE UNSKILLED MANUAL WORKERS HAVE CHANGED THEIR JOBS OR WERE UNEMPLOYED IN THE LAST YEAR

0% OF THESE SEMI-SKILLED MANUAL WORKERS CHANGED THEIR JOBS OR WERE UNEMPLOYED IN THE LAST YEAR

15% OF THESE SKILLED MANUAL WORKERS CHANGED THEIR JOBS OR WERE UNEMPLOYED IN THE LAST YEAR

30% OF THESE WHITE-COLLAR WORKERS CHANGED THEIR JOBS OR WERE UNEMPLOYED IN THE LAST YEAR

It can be seen that over a quarter of the unskilled workers earning less than N.A.W. were unemployed last year. This is worse than any of the other categories of workers, except white-collar workers, especially when considering the Holloway department of employment's figures of unemployment which were declining after the 1965 squeeze and 1966 S.E.T. initiation.

Holloway unemployment

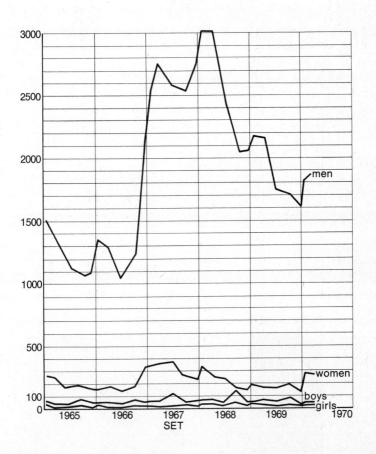

3000

2500

2000 — men

1500

1000

500

300 — women

100 — boys
0 — girls

1965   1966   1967   1968   1969   1970
SET

HOUSEHOLD INCOME MAKE UP < N.A.W.

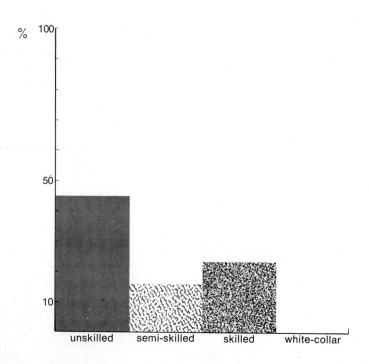

WORKER
INCOME < N.A.W

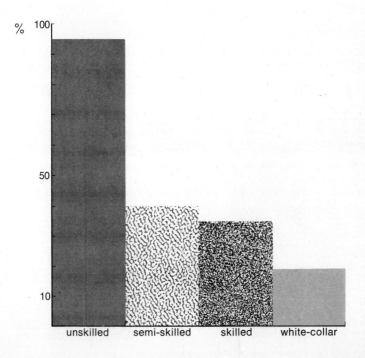

WORKFORCE
EARNING < N.A.W.

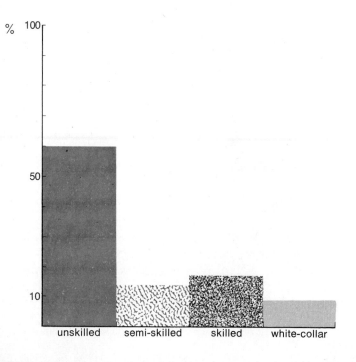

Of the total unskilled manual labour force 95% ARE EARNING LESS THAN N.A.W.

semi-skilled	40%	„	„	„	„	„
skilled	35%	„	„	„	„	„
white collar	19%	„	„	„	„	„

The N.A.W. figures show that material conditions have worsened and economic isolation increased. Seventy per cent of those earning less than N.A.W. who were unemployed in the last year were unskilled manual workers. This was in spite of the fact that they only make up sixty per cent of the workforce in this group. Fifteen per cent of skilled workers and white-collar workers earning less than N.A.W. were unemployed during last year.

95% of all unskilled manual workers are earning less than **N.A.W.**

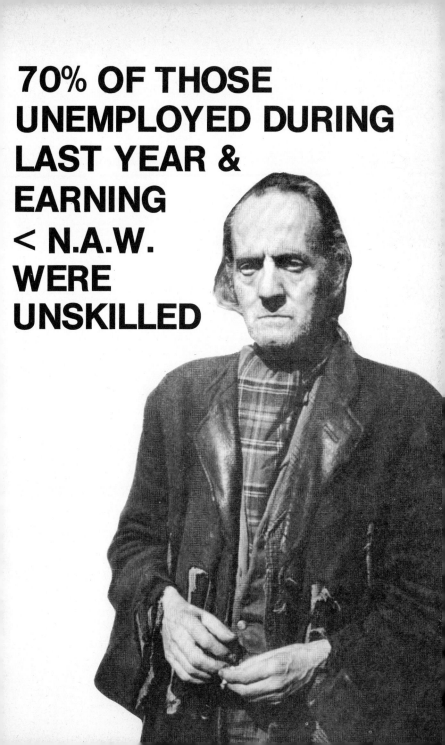

70% OF THOSE
UNEMPLOYED DURING
LAST YEAR &
EARNING
< N.A.W.
WERE
UNSKILLED

average wage for these workers has risen from £8–£12 in five years

WAGES

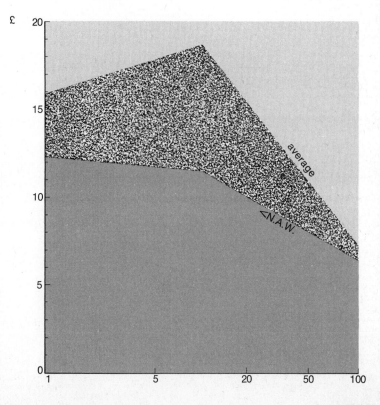

78% of those who job-changed or were unemployed in the last 5 years had been there less than 5 years.

UNSKILLED WORKERS EARNING < N.A.W.

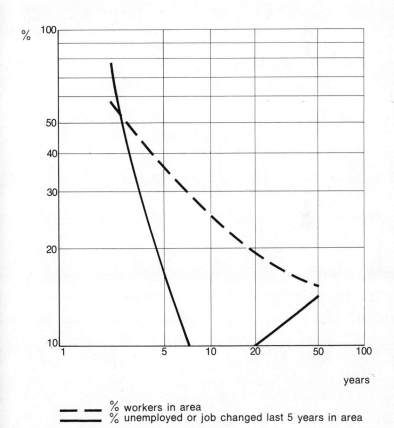

%

years

— — % workers in area
—— % unemployed or job changed last 5 years in area

The average wage for those unskilled workers earning less than N.A.W. (i.e. ninety-five per cent of them) has risen from £8 to £12 in the last five years. This is an increase of fifty per cent, although it is only seventy per cent of N.A.W. Meanwhile the cost of living has risen fifty per cent, and was already above their means five years ago. It must also be remembered that devaluation means that the present day £12 in pre-devaluation terms equals £10. 8s. 0d. Thus wage increase is not fifty per cent, but thirty per cent. So it can be seen that with the standard of living rising and wage increase only twenty-five per cent, they are actually worse off by twenty per cent.

The length of stay in the area was related to the wage situation of those workers earning less than N.A.W.

58% OF THE UNSKILLED WORKERS WERE LIVING IN THE AREA LESS THAN 5 YEARS AND HAD AN AVERAGE WAGE OF £12

26% OF THE UNSKILLED WORKERS WERE LIVING IN THE AREA BETWEEN 5 AND 20 YEARS AND HAD AN AVERAGE WAGE OF £11.13

16% OF THE UNSKILLED WORKERS WERE LIVING IN THE AREA MORE THAN 20 YEARS AND HAD AN AVERAGE WAGE OF £9.4

Of those workers living in the area less than five years the increase in wage was approximately forty-eight per cent. Those living from five to twenty years in the area had an increase in income of about sixty per cent. One of the main reasons for this is that nearly two thirds of this group are working mothers who were not working five years ago. This is important because it reflects consistence among those economically estranged. All along in this survey, it has been shown that those who have lived in the area less than five years or more than twenty years are worse off. Those in the group from five to twenty years have settled down to a steady job and have less unemployment than those newly arrived. Even in this section of the survey which deals with those workers who have an income of less than £17 those who are worst off are the unskilled workers who have been here less than five or more than twenty years. The unskilled workers in the middle group are supplementary earners in the family. The family does not totally rely on them.

Of those unemployed or who had changed jobs in the last five years :
78% had been in the area less than 5 years.
7% had been there between 5 and 20 years
and 15% had been living there over 20 years.

Of this group of unskilled workers:

22%	WERE IN	GLC PROPERTY	OF WHOM	100%	HAD BEEN THERE LESS THAN 5 YEARS					
66%	„	PRIVATE	„	„	„	42%	„	„	„	„ „
12%	„	HOUSING ASS.	„	„	100%	„	„	„	„	„

Of those in private accommodation sixteen per cent had been there between five and twenty years, and forty-two per cent more than twenty years.

The low preponderance (fifteen per cent) of workers who had changed jobs over the last few years and had been living there for more than twenty years suggests a lack of confidence about job changing (either through inability or caution), except when necessary through unemployment or redundancy. It must be realized that of this fifteen per cent perhaps one third are less than thirty years old and have been born in the same house from which they are working. Most of the activity of job changing and unemployment takes place in this younger group.

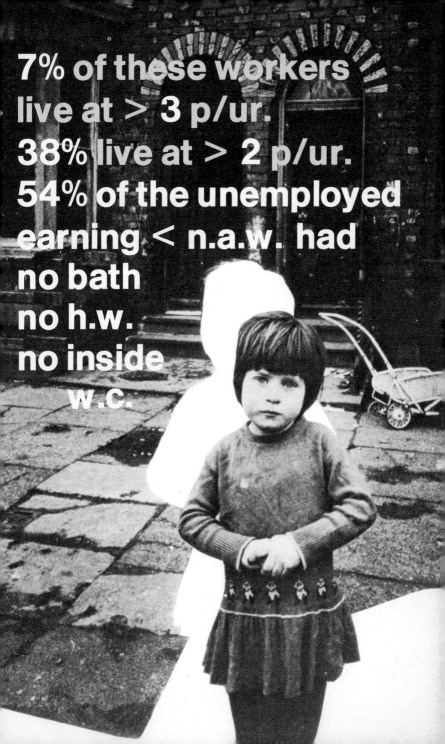

7% of these workers
live at > 3 p/ur.
38% live at > 2 p/ur.
54% of the unemployed
earning < n.a.w. had
no bath
no h.w.
no inside
w.c.

THOSE WITHOUT SANITATION

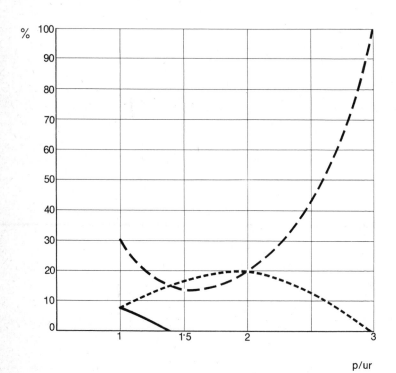

%

p/ur

- — — unskilled
- ······· skilled
- —— white-collar

DENSITY AND FACILITIES

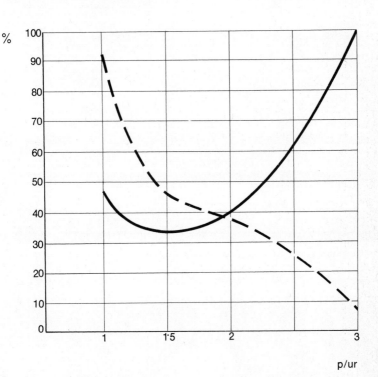

unemployed earning <N.A.W.
no sanitation

Having shown that the worst economic conditions exist for those who were unskilled manual workers, a correlation between bad living conditions and bad job opportunities and wages became apparent.

Of those people who have been unemployed in the last 5 years and are earning less than N.A.W. (which is 40% of this group):

											UNSKILLED WORKERS
7% ARE LIVING AT A DENSITY OF MORE THAN 3 p/ur OF WHOM 100% ARE											
38% ,,	,,	,,	,,	,,	,,	2	,,	,,	,,	60%	,,
46% ,,	,,	,,	,,	,,	,,	1·5	,,	,,	,,	66%	,,
92% ,,	,,	,,	,,	,,	,,	1	,,	,,	,,	75%	,,

As well as living in these overcrowded conditions:

54% HAD NO BATH AND AN OUTSIDE TOILET

If this is broken down even further it is found that:
100% of those living at 3/p/ur had no bath and outside W.C. and were unskilled.

40%	,,	,, ,,	2	,,	,,	,,	,,	,,	50%	,,	,,
33%	,,	,, ,,	1·5	,,	,,	,,	,,	,,	50%	,,	,,
46%	,,	,, ,,	1	,,	,,	,,	,,	,,	66%*	,,	,,

* i.e. 34% were skilled. Half of these were white-collar workers.

Looking at the make-up of those households with an income of less than N.A.W., it can be seen that they have either been there less than five years or more than twenty years. Of those in the former category thirty per cent were living in G.L.C. property (the other seventy per cent were in private property). They were living at an average density of two p/ur whereas those in the private sector were living at 1·25 people p/ur. The average for the total group of households who had been in the area less than five years was 1·4 p/ur.

For the long-established households, those in G.L.C. tenancy (forty-three per cent) had a density of 0·65 p/ur and those in private accommodation were living at 0·9 p/ur. The average for this total group was 0·8 p/ur. The average density at which people were living within all the households with an income of less than N.A.W. was one p/ur.

Sanitary conditions were also correlated with length of stay and tenancy.

% with either no hot water, no bath, an outside toilet or any combination of these:

5 years or less, in G.L.C. tenancy	50%
„ „ „ in private „	40%
Average for this group	43%
More than 20 yrs, in G.L.C. tenancy	100%
„ „ „ in private „	50%
Average for this group	70%
TOTAL AVERAGE	57%

Throughout this survey, bad conditions, overcrowding, lack of basic sanitary necessities, bad job opportunities, low wages, and unemployment have been found to rest, basically, within two sectors of the population of this area; those unskilled workers who have been living in the area for over twenty years or those who have recently arrived. People living in private accommodation suffered most, but there is very little difference between this group and those living in G.L.C. property. They pay more, but live at a slightly lower density; more of them were unemployed during the last five years. The situation for them is getting worse. Many are earning relatively less today than they were five years ago. They are economically alienated. It doesn't matter to the economy whether they work or not. Many do not work and exist on social security. Many are sociologically alienated as well.

⅓ of 400 children in a school were KNOWN to be from disturbed or broken homes. It is suggested that this figure is really ½.

one class had 15 teachers in the first 5 months.

85% of new entrants in last 2 weeks came from THIS BACKGROUND.

5. Social Survey

What they expect in their own situation in any foreseeable future is very little: they may want more, they may believe they have a right to more: but they have learned and they have been brought up to settle for a minimum. Life is like that, they say.

   Their foreseen minimum is not purely economic: it is not even principally economic. Today the minimum might include a car. It is above all an intellectual, emotional and spiritual minimum. It almost empties of content such concepts (expressed in no matter what words) as renewal, sudden change, passion, delight, tragedy, understanding. It reduces sex to a passing urge, effort to what is necessary in order to maintain a status quo, love to kindness, comfort to familiarity. It dismisses the efficacy of thought, the power of unrecognised needs, the relevance of history. It substitutes the notion of endurance for that of experience, of relief for that of benefit.

Peter Berger

Marx believed in the 'universal essence' of man. As has been seen in the previous report, 'self-fulfilment' through productive or creative labour was the goal. He considered it as an existential activity of man, his free conscious activity, not as a means of maintaining life but for developing his universal nature.

The second survey was to check, as best one can, the probable social alienation within this area. Various degrees of alienation were found on a pilot project survey but not enough to be conclusive. A questionnaire was then prepared using the experience gained from the trial survey and this proved to be the final version. The questions were designed to find out the varying and various shades of social alienation as described by Fromm, Merton, Scott and Faunce. So categories such as 'self-estrangement' or 'isolation' were used to describe the responses to a series of environmental pressures whether they be economic, cultural or physical. The most common response to poverty today appears to be alienation.

In industrial societies, the poor are confronted by a 'status assignment' system, in which occupational, economic and educational achievements are the primary basis for differentiating status levels. Self-perpetuating cultural deprivation demonstrates that, in consequence of a low level of school achievement, the child is likely to respond by assigning low reward values to success as a student, and to drop out at the first opportunity. This means that he enters the 'labour market' at a disadvantage, in that the only jobs he is likely to get are those most likely to produce alienation from work. This, as has been shown, is transmitted from one generation to another, especially in isolated or potentially isolated areas.

To escape from this situation involves a process, sociologically described as 'individuation'. This is a break from the communal/community living patterns that had previously been observed. It is relinquishing these patterns to strive for individual achievement goals that enables those living in deprived areas to get out. Those with initiative can do so.

Many try to succeed by aspiring to a higher socio-economic value system, and are 'mobility orientated'. This involves a determined effort or series of efforts to get out of the current situation. Values and norms of a higher socio-economic group are assumed, so that eventually they will be able to better themselves both in material and value terms. If the pressure arising out of the situation is too great, then those people affected, especially those already economically alienated, tend to withdraw and are made to withdraw from society. The first and most common step is 'self-estrangement'. Work no longer provides the opportunity for creative self-expression and so the worker is alienated from the product of his work and the work process; hence 'alienating himself from man'. The activities become meaningless in themselves, but are simply a means to other ends. People work for money to live not because they like work; if they do, it's a bonus instead of a right.

This leads to a sense of 'powerlessness', a loss of control over important decisions and events affecting people's lives. This is especially true with the present increasing growth in the bureaucracy business. It is a form of 'deprivation'. Within industrial society this sense of powerlessness pervades our experience, as do the impersonal forces that produce it. The familiar 'you can't beat the system' is a form of apathy. The ombudsman was originally conceived as having a clientele of citizens who were most likely to experience powerlessness. He himself is powerless in most fields where powerlessness and deprivation exist. Within this 'apathy structure' cynicism and satire grow. Success in one's calling used to be an 'outward sign of inner grace'; wealth was virtue, poverty sin. But the 'early to bed, early to rise' has given rise to 'it's not what you do, but who you know'. The anti-hero is a product of a powerless situation.

The conformity encouraged by this situation, and accepted by many, is a form of 'meaninglessness'. It is difficult to make accurate predictions about the behaviour of others or about the outcome of one's own actions; or with different and changing segments of society, to find the standards regarding courses of action or patterns of belief. But 'routinization', the path of least resistance, with no incentive to deviate or innovate, is present in all parts of the social hierarchy. This is the conformity of 'other-directed' behaviour, the 'organization man' where success or failure at work is measured by efficiency of the department or profitability of the enterprise. For those in 'deprived areas' it is this wish not to be bothered and the lack of initiative and incentive that leave many of them trapped. For those in white-collar organization jobs this leads to a quest for status symbols.

Those who find their efforts frustrated by the 'organization' turn in despair to a situation where there are no effective norms or rules for behaviour. A form of this is 'normlessness'. In contemporary society, there are no legitimate means, on many occasions, to achieve socially prescribed goals. Civil disobedience, crime and delinquency are the answer in many cases. The inability to achieve generally accepted goals through socially approved means implies an illegal alternative as the only way. Those in deprived areas don't even make good criminals. So a person withdraws, and part of the symptom is isolation from society. This leads to a giving of low reward values to goals or beliefs that are typically highly held in society, such as education, the need to work etc.

What suffers here is the 'self-image'. Personal values, and major values that shape our personalities are a social product. If, as has been suggested, we always need the poor to be able to keep our self-image as a part of society, then it should be recognized that the poor and those living below the poverty line also need their

101

'self-maintenance'. To be certain that we are what we think we are, we need some periodical confirmation of this fact from others. The social test of self-esteem involves acting in ways that 'others' would approve, even though they are not present to observe the actions. Thus with continual lack of confirmation, and continual bombardment of the fact that they are working class, ignorant and lazy, those in the deprived areas tend to reinforce their physical environment with an invisible social environment. The maintenance of self-esteem then either disappears or is refocused on activities that are relevant to the area, such as football.

This status hierarchy develops where there is an unequal distribution of 'goodies' and the intrinsic value of the job is repaid by unequal extrinsic rewards. Thus a nurse has work of high intrinsic value but very low extrinsic gain; a doctor receives both value and gain.

Every stable set of human interrelationships, whether it be within the family, friends, community, or a total society, has an identifiable status structure. The hierarchy of people is based on the extent to which they are accorded social honour. This leads to differences in the unequal distribution of anything that is valued. Thus in work there is an unequal distribution of skill, responsibility and authority; and a person is regarded as 'low status' on some dimension that he does not use in evaluating himself.

We are alienated from others or from any organization in which we are a member to the extent that the criteria we use to evaluate ourselves are different from the criteria used by others in evaluating us.   *Faunce*

Thus a worker in a factory is not motivated to major organizational goals. This means, in many cases, a feeling of failure and a lowering of status, as well as a lowering of aspirations; a person will conserve his energies for what he regards as more important. Within a community or (as in many decaying or deprived areas) a non-community, an individual is aware of his immediate social environment and his attitudes are shaped by these 'shared values' and 'shared goals'. Close social relations are based on these values, and there is a process of identification and commitment to achieve the objectives and goals of those in a higher socio-economic group, thus ensuring social status and confirmation of self-assessment. There tends to be little identification, except with negative objectives, in a 'deprived' area.

With the continual rationalization of society the capacity of people to think independently decreases. 'Substantial rationality' is the decline in the extent to which people are able to see interrelations among events that affect them and act intelligently on the basis of this insight. The ability to arrive at their own judgements has decreased. The complexity and segmentation of society has also helped to mould a 'silent majority' or, in the case of deprived areas, 'silent minority'. Social roles and self-identities are isolated, leading to an increase in the difficulty of understanding meaningful interrelationships among events.

These were the questions asked of householders in the second survey:

1. Where did you come from?
2. Why did you come to this area?
3. Are you disappointed in what you found here, if so, what are you disappointed about and why? if not, why is your answer as it is?
4. Do you think you can get a better job by going to evening classes?
5. Do you think you will have your job in five years' time? if not, what sort of job do you think you will be doing?
6. What do you think your children will do when they grow up?
7. If you could get a job for more money, but in a different part of the country or in a foreign country, would you go?
8. Do you think your job is important and helps others?
9. Do you like your work, or would you prefer a different job?
10. If you don't like your work, why do you do it?
11. Are you trying to get a higher position in your job, if so why?
12. How do you think people who have more money than you, got it?
13. If you could get the same amount of money in three days' work what would you do for the rest of the week?
14. If you are going to have a lot of free time off work, do you think you should be taught (at school) things that you could do during your free time?
15. What do you do when you are not working?
16. Do you think your children are getting, or got, as good an education as children who came from middle-class or upper-class areas?
17. If not, why not, and whose fault is it?

18. If you were given the choice (and money) would you send your children to a grammar school or public school?
19. Do you think they are getting the right sort of education – if not, what do you think is the right sort?
20. Who are your heroes?
21. Do you believe what you see on T.V. and read in the papers?
22. What sort of things have you seen advertised that you have bought?
23. If you won £500 what would you do with it?
24. What do you think of policemen and why?
25. Would you like to be able to have more say in things that affect your life?
26. What is your local M.P. for and do you think he does his job properly?
27. If not, do you think you should do something on your own or with a group of people, and are you prepared to do so?
28. Would you ever demonstrate or barricade yourself in your house, if you felt you were right in your protest?
29. Does everyone feel like this in this area?
30. Do you think you should have a better place to live – if so where and why?
31. What do you think of the different classes?
    a) working class
    b) middle class
    c) upper class
32. Would you rather be in another class and why?
33. Do you think the area you live in affects your way of life?
34. Do you know many people in this area?
35. What do you think you can do best?
36. What would you like to be?
37. What would you like your children to be when they grow up?
38. Is there anything you'd like to tell me or say to me?
39. Have you a car?

Because the survey was limited, both in size, time and control, only inferences can be made as to the values, norms and roles of the various participants. In this part of the survey a selection of people from a typical middle-class area in north London were interviewed as a 'value-check'. I also had the opportunity to interview the residents of Hillside reception centre for the homeless, who are included in the survey of the area.

There tend to be differences in values between the 'classes'.

Class in this case is judged by values and norms held. These range from middle class (MC), middle class aspirants (MCA) to working class (WC), 'residual classes' (RC), and combinations of adjacent value systems.

The survey was followed up by case studies of several people in the area. This involved not only long personal interviews and discussions but also trying to understand through the social workers some of the problems involved in the area in order to see various aspects of the 'reality' that people were living.

For the sake of brevity only a few examples and cases of social alienation and non-alienation will be demonstrated, to act as a comparison and guide lines. The interviews and report are in the form of case histories rather than statistics, which tend to impress only statisticians. Where considered necessary, though, they will be incorporated. It should be remembered that the terms used here are sociological shorthand for an essentially urban industrial phenomenon. They are not to be used as a diagnostician's countdown but rather as a pointer to various behaviour patterns that are common to a group of people as seen from the middle-class liberal sociologist's viewpoint.

of those
'alienated'

'... I AM THE LOWEST, RIGHT DOWN IN THE GUTTER ...'

66%   were unskilled

85%   earning < N.A.W

100%   in area < five years

Case One

Mrs A. came from Jamaica with the prospect of bettering her life both materially and culturally. She and her husband were at first reasonably successful, they had middle-class aspirations for their children and their standard of living. But through a series of events she finds herself much worse off. She still retains some MC values; for instance she is worried about the children regressing, but doesn't seem to want to do anything about it.(1) She was offered a house in Yorkshire by the housing association who are now providing her present flat, but total despair has taken hold.(2) Her husband, an unskilled labourer, is about to be made redundant. She cannot afford not to work even though most of her wages go on tax and fares.(3) Previous MCA problems left over with H.P. problems. Her attitude to the rich tended towards the negative, inferring that she was a failure, i.e. they got their money by winning it.(4) She was hesitant towards the children with aspirations for them as professionals with a good education. She realized the significance of the home environment as an essential part of learning. There were no books. The children could not get into school as it was already overcrowded.

Her despair had infiltrated down to the point of saying 'I am the lowest, right down in the gutter, below working class', when asked about her thoughts on the various classes.(5) Attitudes to what she could do best were alienated from herself; she saw herself in her role and as others saw her.(6) Both she and her husband do nothing in their spare time and would do the same for a three-day week.(7) Her husband spends money on horses and dogs and other non-participatory recreations. He escapes from the house as often as possible because of domestic strains. This, of course, affects her, as can be seen by her fantasy heroes. Her attitude to authority was one of total resignation and she answered negatively on decision making.(8) Her passivity was reinforced by her belief in events on T.V.(9) However positive her aspirations were for her children's future she replied negatively on opportunities of evening classes.(10) Her job was not important, it was only to get money for her family.(11)

1. Deprivation (non-control over facilities)
2. Deprivation/lack of mobility orientation
3. Self-estrangement
4. Status structure

5. Self-esteem maintenance/status structure (lack of role organization)
6. Status structure
7. Deprivation (non-commitment to values)
8. Powerlessness/meaninglessness
9. Lack of substantial rationality
10. Isolation (non-commitment to values)
11. Self-estrangement.

Case Two

Mr Z. was put in his house by the G.L.C., hoping to be rehoused. He is relatively young and has the potential initiative to move out, but isn't interested. His only criticism of the area was the bad housing conditions he was living in. Windows were broken and left unrepaired but, as the house was rented, he refused to pay for the damages which were part of his bad housing conditions. He has an unskilled manual job. He reckons he is unlikely to have the same job in five years' time, and doesn't even know if it will be labouring; nevertheless it is likely to be unskilled, and he is uninterested in promotion.(1) He only works for the money.(2) Although satisfied with the present situation is earning less than N.A.W. His attitude to money is one of self-failure.(3) He would bank the money although he has no bank, and not use the opportunity to move out. He responded negatively to questions about the future of his children. (This question offers him the opportunity to recreate his life chances for himself in the guise of helping his children.(4) The fact that he spends most of his free time in the betting shop reflects his attitude to money. He would do the same if on a three day week.(5)

He is uninterested in, and apathetic about, possible home improvements, or learning new skills in either education and leisure.(6) Although he evinced interest in evening classes as a help in getting a better job, he himself will not go. He is against demonstrating or protesting about his rights for purely apathetic reasons, 'it won't do no good'.(7) His attitude towards law was ambivalent. His attitude to the class question was more MCA. This is not backed up by action or aspirations to MCA values, such as attaining promotion, better education or more money.(8) Similarly, as has been said before, he wouldn't spend time or money on his present housing situation, relying on the G.L.C.

to house the family; so he's just sitting in very bad conditions and waiting. He sees no connection between a bad environment, such as his own house, and its effects on life. Neither does he recognize the community or non-community in the area; he contradicted himself in two questions about his knowledge of what people do, feel or think in this area.(9)

1. Lack of mobility orientation
2. Self-estrangement
3. Status structure
4. Isolation (lack of shared values)
5. Meaningless/lack of mobility orientation
6. Deprivation/isolation
7. Meaninglessness/powerlessness
8. Lack of substantial rationality
9. Lack of substantial rationality

Case Three

Mr X. was housed by the G.L.C. welfare departments after not being able to find a house or flat.(1) He is disappointed with the conditions of the area, not in terms of lack of educational or cultural facilities but of leisure amenities. He is an unskilled manual worker and has been unemployed several times. He is not interested in promotion.(2) He expects to have the same job for the next few years, and is alienated from his work by not liking it and doing it only for the money.(3) Yet he is not interested in moving out to a better area.(4)

'The rich got their money by living off the poor or by inheritance' were the main reasons he gave when asked about his attitude to those who had more money than he. This is, as has been shown, a reflection of self-failure.(5) When asked what he would do with money he decided to spend it on house necessities and bank the rest; he wishes eventually to be independent. He reacted in a negative way to the learning of new skills.(6) He tended to be more of a spectator than a participator and so is not interested in leisure except in terms of T.V. and watching football. If given a three-day week he would continue to watch football and would probably play. It was only as an afterthought that he mentioned looking for a better place to live (that seemed to be for my benefit).

His attitude to his children's education and what he envisaged for them was negative.(7) He didn't have much confidence in the education authorities because he resented discipline in his youth and had an unhappy school life. He had truancy records. He was ambivalent about authority, but the despair caused by his conditions and the frustrations of being at the end of the G.L.C. line made him quite willing to take part in civil disobedience, such as barricading himself in his house.(8) He identified with the working class to the extent of calling the middle class snobs. No attempt would be made with his money to get a new place although the conditions he was living in left much to be desired. It was for this reason that his heroes, or the people that he admired, were 'Shelter' — they could make things better for him.(9)

1. Powerlessness (non-control over facilities)
2. Lack of mobility orientation
3. Self-estrangement
4. Lack of mobility orientation
5. Status structure
6. Isolation (non-commitment to values)
7. Isolation
8. Normlessness
9. Status structure

Case Four

This woman has been continually on the move, so that no place disappoints her.(1) She is not working and subsists on social security, family allowances and whatever she can get in terms of free handouts.(2) She has no husband, she has three children. She once wanted to be a hairdresser but has never really wanted to work and has no initiative to better herself economically or otherwise.(3) Her attitude to money and the rich is MCA; she would get a place if she managed to get hold of a reasonable sum of money. Although she wanted her son to be a doctor, and to go to a grammar school, she made no attempt to educate him as she had never stayed more than six months at one place.(4) The last place she stayed at was in Birmingham; before that Scotland. Her son had never been properly educated and she accepted no responsibility in this field. There were no books and she rarely participated in activities with the children. Her leisure activities were taken up by eating, smoking, and sleeping.(5)

These 'fantasy' attitudes and visions were confirmed by her passive fantasy attitude to T.V. Her attitude to learning was negative.(6)

As for authority, when she came into contact with it, she just moved on. There was a sense of great despair, she wouldn't demonstrate or take action, but packed her bags and moved out.(7) Her 'self-image' was completely crushed. She was 'no good at anything'.(8) She had no heroes or no one she could identify with but, unlike those with middle-class values (who tend to see themselves as their own heroes) there was a listlessness. She was not 'worthy' to identify herself with anyone.(9) She had nothing to say about the class question, not because she was aspiring to the middle class, but because she basically did not know how people other than herself lived.(10) She was aware of her environment and its consequences on her children, but she still kept on the go. 'Nowhere disappoints me.'

 1. Isolation (non-commitment to values)
 2. Lack of shared values
 3. Lack of mobility orientation
 4. Lack of substantial rationality
 5. Deprivation/meaninglessness (non-commitment to values)
 6. Isolation
 7. Powerlessness/deprivation (non-control over facilities)
 8. Self-esteem maintenance (lack of role organization)
 9. Lack of shared values/goals/self-esteem maintenance
10. Lack of substantial rationality

Case Five (*Potential*)

He has been transferred by the council twice to this area; the situation was completely out of his hands.(1) His only disappointments were not in terms of the conditions he was living in, both physically and economically, as he was unaware of environmental effects, but from a leisure point of view.(2) He is an unskilled worker who has been unemployed within the last year. He had a conventional attitude to work and education, and was in favour of bettering oneself. His attitude to his children was positive; he saw them in a secure position but in a very limited fashion – not as would most aspirants, in terms of professional jobs, but in terms of government and public service industries which were pensionable and secure. His attitude to his job was more negative. He wasn't interested in moving on or trying to get promoted.(3) He was 'secure' in his job, although he disliked it and did it only for the money.(4) The rich 'nicked' their money (a reflection on himself) yet if he were given £500 he would spend it all, and have a 'splash'. Normally in his spare time he did nothing and would continue to do so if he had a three-day week.(5)

In fact, he was a bit of a fascist (remember Hannah Arendt) in his attitude to immigrants and education. This was confirmed by the fact that his heroes fitted into this pattern, being disciplinarians, and his respect and admiration for these figures accounted for his almost forelock-touching attitude to the 'upper class'. He was anti-authority in terms of personal rights and was determined to demonstrate, especially against immigrants. When asked about class, he replied as would a MCA, but then qualified this response by answering unfavourably about the middle class.(6)

1. Powerlessness (non-control of facilities)
2. Lack of substantial rationality
3. Lack of mobility orientation
4. Self-estrangement
5. Self-esteem maintenance (lack of role organization)
6. Status structure.

Case Six (Non-Alienated)

Mr P. came to this area for no particular reason, other than to work. He could only get housing through the housing association. He is an unskilled manual worker, and although he likes his job he probably won't have it in five years' time. His new job will be more skilled as he is continually acquiring new skills. He has already had promotion and is trying for more. Although he does not consider his job directly helpful to people or even important, he is interested in the possibilities of better positions as he becomes more skilled.

He has already moved but would move again if this meant better prospects. His attitudes to education were positive. He was interested in his children, in their learning and upbringing, and spends his leisure time with them. He was satisfied with the sort of education they were getting at school and, compared with

Ceylon, from where he came, they were far better off. His imagination was limited but this seems to be because he has only recently immigrated. His attitude to leisure was positive, he spent time around the house with the children and, if given a three-day week, would probably get another job. His attitude to authority was MCA; there are proper channels for civil disobedience and, as an immigrant, he is in a very vulnerable position. On being asked about class he replied as an aspirant, preferring to move to an area where there were a better class of immigrants. He considers his present housing situation bad, although his house is one of the better ones in the area.

Case Seven (Non-Alienated)

Mr Y. came to London to get work. He knew that the conditions he would have to put up with were bad, and expected them. But he was more than disappointed about the educational facilities for his children. He is a white-collar worker who likes his job, but reckons that within five years he will be self-employed. He has been promoted, and is angling for a more responsible position. If this involved moving he would do so. As for money, he would spend it on qualitative items, both in terms of the house and culture. His attitude to the rich reflected his own aspirations.

On the education side he was very positive, being engaged in the arts fields and spending his time and leisure with the children, taking them out, showing them places. His attitude to authority was perceptive. The MP was not his representative as he himself has no representation. He has become apathetic to the whole problem of bureaucracy, especially as he believes that local government democracy does not exist. Areas such as these should be run on non-political grounds so that the people living in them are not treated as pawns in a political game. He gave a typical aspirant's answer to the problem of class consciousness. The area, he considered, could be better used. There were existing resources, such as empty houses, that could easily be used for the homeless in London. He was aware of environmental defects in the area both from a physical and from a social point of view.

These examples, drawn from the survey, seek to illustrate the differences between those sociologically alienated, those potentially alienated and those conforming to the norms of their own value systems. Out of the thirty-two interviews in this part of the survey it can be inferred that:

```
    18% WERE SOCIOLOGICALLY ALIENATED
     6% WERE POTENTIALLY ALIENATED
(OF WHOM 66% WERE OF A WORKING-CLASS/RESIDUAL CLASS VALUE
                                                      SYSTEM)
    66% OF THOSE SOCIOLOGICALLY ALIENATED WERE UNSKILLED
    17%    ,,      ,,         ,,          ,,        ,,      SEMI-SKILLED
    17%    ,,      ,,         ,,          ,,        ,,      UNEMPLOYED
OF THOSE POTENTIALLY ALIENATED 100% WERE UNSKILLED MANUAL
    WORKERS
    85% OF THOSE ALIENATED WERE EARNING LESS THAN N.A.W.
   100%    ,,      ,, POTENTIALLY ALIENATED WERE EARNING LESS THAN N.A.W.
OF THOSE SOCIOLOGICALLY ALIENATED:
    34% WERE LIVING IN PRIVATE ACCOMMODATION
    50%    ,,       ,, ,, G.L.C. OR COUNCIL PROPERTY
    16%    ,,       ,, ,, HOUSING ASSOCIATIONS
OF THOSE SOCIOLOGICALLY ALIENATED:
   100% HAD BEEN THERE LESS THAN 5 YEARS
    50% OF THOSE POTENTIALLY ALIENATED HAD BEEN THERE LESS THAN 5
       YEARS AND
    50% HAD BEEN THERE BETWEEN 5 AND 20 YEARS
```

It can be seen by these figures, albeit only inferences from the survey, that a substantial minority group is not only economically isolated but sociologically as well. Most are unskilled, earning less than N.A.W., and have lived in the area for less than five years. It can be assumed from this that the situation was almost non-existent five years ago. The families interviewed were not problem families, as has been shown by ten cases of mentally or emotionally disturbed families. The situation will get worse due to exterior pressures (see main report). The problem today is relatively minor and occurs only in 'isolated' areas in urban centres. But unless it is looked into, it will deteriorate. The Child Poverty Action Group report indicates this. The Race Relations Board indicates this. Both put most emphasis on the economic ghettoes and deprived areas, the places where the 'no chance' people live.

Conversations with a School Headmaster

Q. This is a so-called 'deprived area'. What is the effect on education; are there any special facilities or books?

A. These kids come from homes where education is not considered important. They do not live in a 'reading environment'. There are no books and the only reading material is magazines my works unto the end, to him will I give *power over the nations*: And he shall *rule* them with a rod of iron" (Rev. 2:26-27).

For some, this "power over the nations" is going to involve [...] over cities. This is shown by the parable of the pou[...] the 19[...] parable exa[...] whip[...] or ten cities is given to those who qualify. Th[...] duce more are given greater rewards (verses 16-[...] those who fail [...] pro- duce anything receive less reward[...] 20-27).

God is g[...] to po[...] row's mayors [...] those who [...] positions of rulership over cities. For more detail[...] God's Government as it will be in the World Tomorrow, write for our free booklet, *The Wonderful World Tomorrow — [...] It Will Be Like.*

Tomorrow[...]

Spirit Beings who are God. And *how* will they rule? Why, with all the resources of wisdom, understanding, love, might and POWER of the God-Family!

[...] These rulers won't cater to some [...] in [...] als [...] nse of others. They won't be influenced in the least by petty politics. Their [...] be[...]

They won't fear being thrown out of [...] rough [...] will possess the power to swiftly put down any self-exalting, rebellious [...]

Neither will these rulers tolerate [...] and degeneracy. [...] when the lower classes are put in new apartments and schools by the government, what happens? Do these people appreciate what they are given? [...] ases. NO! In a period of

months many new facilities have fixtures stolen, doors and windows are broken, the smell of urine may even be detected in halls and elevators and the whole place is a *wreck!*

[...] mo[...] es people will be taught that this is not the way to live. [...] ill [...] ly not be *allowed* to be lo[...] egenerate. Those who *insist* on being that way will be pun[...] ed so swiftly and surely that they will learn very quickly. And all will head and fear[...]

[...] row's mayors are going to *force* their subjects to obey God and to re[...] e [...] ss [...] will impose a [...] e that will bring *compulsory joy!* They will *insist* on happiness for their citizens. They will *demand* plenty and goodness in their lives. And they will COMMAND them to be healthy, and filled with a sense of well-being and contentment!

And most of these subjects will

"... 'We are gods and we can dictate to you.' This may be great for the First National Bank, but it's worthless when people are concerned."

like *Weekend* or tabloid newspapers like the *Sun*. The effect of T.V. on the vocabulary is tremendous, and leads to a lowering of academic standards. One could call this place a 'cultural desert'.

People don't know what to do to get out of this situation. They struggle to exist in economic terms. Overcrowded tenements and the probability that most of the parents are unskilled or semi-skilled and often unemployed, does not encourage a good educational background. No professional people send their children here. I suppose it's to do with the housing situation; Islington has one of the largest housing problems.

Children are from a more 'permissive' background, there is more responsibility and this funnily enough tends to end up in vandalism. The kids wander around more freely, life is more competitive, kids are tougher and fight harder. Violence is just under the surface; we even have our own extortion rackets going, where one group of boys will demand, 'with menaces', the pocket-money of others. But then if they are not tough here they get trampled into the ground by their competitors. This is why they are good at 'contact sports'. These allow much of their energy to be channelled a little more constructively. But it also means that the teachers have to be strong.

Q. We were dealing before with 'cultural deprivation', but what is the effect of their 'physical deprivation', in terms of environment, effect on their education?

A. The children's diets are not very well regulated, some having to rely on school for their only meal of the day. This affects them in terms of growth and as you may have noticed, they are much smaller for their age than middle-class children.

They seem to have a large amount of pocket-money which goes mostly on eatable things such as sweets or crisps. The impact of the home on physical life varies, but most children lack average benefits and facilities. Their mothers say they cannot control the child, and this seems to be because of their own over-compensation. The children on the other hand are very lively, not easily suppressed and very difficult to encourage.

Q. You would have, I assume, a few 'problem' families in this area; what is the effect on the children? are there any special educational problems?

A. We consider the child can be coped with here, and there are children of 'problem' families in this school. But you must remember that, in an area where the pressures are not much, these children would be getting special help. We have monthly Welfare Meetings where certain children are discussed and priority treatment is recommended. The maladjustment of children is a serious problem in this school; this is of course a relative situation. Many children whom we do not consider maladjusted would be considered so in other situations. Therefore the child has to be so maladjusted that this is of serious concern to the class situation. About one third of the 400 children here were *known* to be from disturbed or broken homes, and with the 'hidden ones', those not known for a fact, this is easily likely to be about half of our school, that is 200 children. Ten out of twelve new entrants in the last two weeks were from disturbed or broken homes. The turnover of pupils is about ten to twelve per cent from September to February; about forty to forty-five children.

For the infants in school there are educational problems. In normal homes, parents have time to talk to the kids. There is a question and answer situation. Here, many parents don't have the opportunity because both are working and get home tired. For instance, there was a girl who was frequently late. It was assumed that there was not enough effort on her part and she was continuously told off. It was then discovered that one of the reasons she was late was that I would talk to her; she was getting some attention. Getting attention sometimes becomes violent. Many times furniture is thrown around in the classroom. There is not much affection at home, and if the mother is aware of this lack then this makes the situation worse; but understanding a child presupposes education. There is a great need for social training.

As for the physical problems, West Indians are very much advanced in all physical athletics except swimming, I don't know why this is, but I understand that there is research going on about this problem. The children are very inhibited about their bodies. They mature quickly and many reach puberty before they are eleven years old. They seem very reluctant to undress. This is probably due to inhibitions about sex in their background. Many have had to live in the same room as their parents and see them 'fighting with no clothes on'. Girls put a lot of clothes on, and it is not uncommon for a girl to have on two vests, a slip, a bodice, two pairs of tights etc. So it can be seen that working-class girls are not as free as supposed. This may be due to ethnic differences within the school. Those of West Indian origin are very open. They have a loose family set up; the parents might leave their children with their family in the West Indies while they come over here to make it. In many instances, a period of years will pass before the children are sent for. During this time the mother might be living with another man and already have two or three children born here. This situation often leads to emotional disturbance for the newly arrived child. Families of Greek origin are very closed. Girls want to behave like British girls but are not allowed to, and all the favours go to the boys who are given greater freedom. The most stable families are the Greek Cypriots and the Indian and Pakistani families.

Q. You mention the problems of ethnic differences; are there many immigrant children in this school and what is the ratio to British children? Are there any special problems that you have to deal with such as discrimination or problems of language?

A. In this area we are into the second generation. Most of the coloured children are not immigrants. In fact the percentage has dropped in the past two years from fifty-two per cent to thirty-five per cent according to the Department of Education and Science (D.E.S.). The kids come from the West Indies, Guyana, India, Pakistan, Mauritius, Kenya, Ghana, Nigeria, Turkey, Cyprus and Greece. There is a high percentage of Irish but these are not considered immigrants.

But this is the crunch. The families with greater initiative move out and their place is taken by those with more difficulties. These new incomers consolidate with the old residue population to form a sort of 'descending spiral'. Here another factor comes into play; eventually, the G.L.C. redevelopment, whenever that will be, will bring a greater stability.

Discrimination is not considered an important issue here. We have a full-time English teacher to teach English to immigrants as a second language, but there are too many to deal with, in groups of a dozen at a time.

Q. What is the turnover of both teachers and pupils in the school? How many children are there in a class, and how well are the staff known?

A. Depending on the class, there are thirty-five to forty children. We have a staff of sixteen of whom six or thirty-seven per cent are leaving. Last year nearly fifty per cent left. This year we started with two teachers short, one class had fifteen different teachers in the first five months of this scholastic year. How well known can one teacher be? But you must pay people more to teach in such areas. Not only is more money needed but more teachers are required. The D.E.S. gives a small amount to the school as it is in a 'priority area', but what use is such a small sum. What is needed is an injection of large sums of money. Plowden doesn't cost anything and the Educational Priority Area allowance is of no effect. More money per head must be made available. Improvements in the premises and supplementary allowances to purchase books are also needed, but I have no complaints as regards facilities. Funnily enough, there was more money for primary education under the Tories; whether this was due to a reluctance for comprehensive schooling I don't know, but it meant we had a good staffing ratio.

Q. With this area being a 'priority area' and with the pressure on classroom space so great, do you find you have any problems with children who are found to be educationally sub-normal? Do you accept them into this school because they have nowhere else to go; if so, do you have a quota? Do you generally have any problems relating to what one might call intelligence, and do these cases refer back to physical conditions at home or in the environment, or are they due to damage at birth?

A. The Inner London Education Authority (I.L.E.A.) has done research into this problem. At this school, academic standards are lower than the norm. I don't think this is because of lower intelligence; nevertheless, the children rarely, if ever, achieve their full potential. They don't get real opportunities, at least not equal opportunities, and so they don't get out of this area.

As for the educationally sub-normal (E.S.N.), a decision is made by a psychologist, and the child is sent to a special school. We've had children who are E.S.N. and I should think this runs into the region of six per year. E.S.N. families tend to reproduce themselves. There are not many places in this area for them to go. We would not accept the child if he or she was E.S.N. but we sometimes hold them in school until they can be placed in a special E.S.N. school. It's hard to understand how it happens, but in this area children aged ten to eleven can be found to be E.S.N. after having been in school for years.

I had better explain that an E.S.N. child suffers from a lack of mental development. It tends to be hereditary, and not occur because of the environment. This environment does not produce more E.S.N.s, but the 'lower ability classes' move into areas such as these. Those with more initiative move away. Perhaps the answer is in improved housing, which is environmental, but you must not confuse environment and low ability. A better environment means greater stimulation for the child and this helps a child of any ability to approach his potential. Thus middle-class and working-class kids have the same lack of abilities, but the middle class will be better off due to the stimulus of their particular environment.

Q. Is there any parent participation in the school, or any adult use of the premises?

A. We are, in fact, just about to start a P.T.A. Parents are always invited for personal interviews about their children, or the curriculum; but there seems to be a lack of contact with other people. Many don't know what goes on in the school, and don't consider it to be part of their responsibility. They compartmentalize their lives so that they are responsible when the child is at home but not when at school. They tend to have short-term objectives and there is an attitude of 'live for the moment'. They want their kids to benefit educationally, but they don't want to be involved and they don't realize that they have to be involved in the child's upbringing. They want grammar schooling but don't realize what's involved. The result is a substantial number of grammar school dropouts from this area.

Adults use the school at night as a play centre and junior club with the children. These play clubs are run by the I.L.E.A. on an informal basis from 4.00 to 6.30 p.m. for junior kids outside school hours, usually until their parents return from work; but I'm not involved in this. There is unfortunately no attempt to get kids and parents to work together; I personally want to see participation developed.

Q. Do you think an opting in, opting out, educational system would be better suited to an area such as this?

A. This is a waste, both on a personal and national level. It is very inefficient, though in fact the same occurs here except it is within the school. When compulsory education was initiated, the working class didn't want it, there were even strikes. The problem is a clash between personal freedom and a 'cruel to be kind' attitude. We have compulsory education, but there are kids we rarely see and this leads to a retarded, backward society made up of 'feckless families'. The great danger in breaking up the compulsory education system is that the privileged classes would benefit even more.

Q. Can 'deprived' children cope with more independent group teaching practices? How does this affect their self-confidence in communication, and do you find that the bad environment affects their concentration?

A. The teachers' interpretations are very different. At this school a child progresses at his own rate. As for group teaching, this depends on the teacher's personality. The kids are doing independent work; some use T.V. and the library as information sources and follow-up using visual equipment. They talk about it, write about it and are self-confident and articulate within their own limitations. There are, as always, periods of concentration and periods of non-concentration.

There is a great percentage of emotional immaturity which tends to lead to a 'pseudo sophistication'. Many are used to having their own way at home nearly all the time and this leads to inconsistencies in their treatment. If a child conforms it will do what is expected and this could be to test the teacher for weaknesses. There are many non-conforming kids in these areas and these children usually have the most interesting personalities.

Q. How far does the school replace the background the children haven't got, or is it meant to? Does it, in fact, set out to change their way of life, by diminishing or increasing interest in the environment?

A. We try to expose them to new experiences in the widest sense. The fundamental tools are communication and social relationships. We expose them to literature, music and culture that they don't experience at home. Most important are the contacts the child makes within the home environment. They meet and socialize only with persons of similar limited experiences. All other experiences are artificial, through the media of T.V. and tabloids. There is no talking in depth and the scope of knowledge is very limited. In fact they tend to consciously limit their own environmental experience. They attempt no contacts outside their own. Those who make it tend to cut the ties with their family.

We do set out to change this way of life. What positive qualities have they got that we can expand or extend? They are open and generous (with their own and other's property). They have a traditional attitude to women; but women seem more interested in education, maybe because dad is at work. You must remember that the working class is paid by the hour. One must search around for their qualities though I find it difficult as I, myself, come from a working-class background.

The middle class has a greater investment in the community. Communities exist where people have spare time, not time between one employment and another. Here, if people have any spare time, and that's a big if, they relax. Leaders are thrown up in middle-class areas but here those with any initiative have gone away.

Q. Can you see, from your position, how a child from this area will fare in the future; is it a foregone conclusion?

A. It's not a foregone conclusion. The greatest development likely to affect them is the decade following school life. This period is very significant because at this point they gain most of their responsibilities, attitudes and emotions. But if no progress is made at school there is likely to be slow progress outside. You could almost say they are 'no chance people' but you can't write them off altogether.

This is perhaps the fault of the system. I would like to see, from an educational standpoint, an injection of high quality teachers, suitably reimbursed when teaching in schools such as this. Intensive research and considerably more money is needed, otherwise the likelihood is that things will continue as they are and people will find it very difficult to get out of their situation. Society is more affluent and not as crude as it used to be.

Q. Have you got any criticism of the present system, with regard to special problems of a priority area such as this?

A. More money, a higher calibre of teacher and a means of maintaining staff mobility, say with high supplementary benefits. In unsavoury situations, as in this area, there should be no problem with money. Selective schools get about thirty or forty applicants for a job. I advertise and I'm lucky to get two, aah well!

10 CASE HISTORIES

Ten Pressure Cases

Case One

Family of six.
Living in two rooms – density of three persons per usable room (3 p/ur).
Father unskilled worker.
Very bad housing conditions, damp, no hot water, no bath, no inside toilet.
Psychosomatic illnesses.
Two children on red alert.
Pressures for rehousing affecting the mental conditions of both parents and children, mother being treated with drugs because of this.

Case Two

Family of five.
Living in two rooms – density of 2·5 p/r.
Father unskilled worker and unemployed.
Very bad housing conditions, damp, no hot water, no bath, no inside toilet.
Psychosomatic illnesses.
One child at risk – backward.
Landlord evicted family because of overcrowding.
Rent Tribunal gave them six months, but because of pressures they will have to be taken into Hillside. They have to wait for the bailiffs to come if they are to have a chance of a house.
Children on the street.

Case Three

Family of seven.
Living in three rooms – density of 2·3 p/r.
Father unskilled – doesn't work.
Very bad housing conditions, damp, no hot water, no bath, no inside toilet.
Physical illnesses of children due to damp.
Last child spastic – on red alert.
Council will not act until child is one year old.
Cannot move out.
No playspace – children not allowed out on streets – this has affected children.

One clinging child.
Physical situation has led to frustrations with no outlets —
emotional disturbances have resulted.
Mother and children mutually neurotic.

Case Four

Family of eight.
Living in two rooms — density of 4 p/r.
Very bad housing conditions, rising sewage causing damp to one
room, family can only use one room, and are therefore living at
density of 8 p/ur. No hot water, no bath, no inside toilet.
Father had affair — led to wife deciding to get pregnant,
hypertension, and eventually a hysterectomy.
Eldest child sleeps out.
Public health authority has condemned house.
Private landlord refuses to do anything.
Mother suffers from hallucinatory aberrations of coffins.

Case Five

Family of five.
Living in 3·5 rooms — density of 1·4 p/r.
Very bad housing conditions, damp, no hot water, no bath, no
inside toilet.
Father always out of work — unskilled.
Rent arrears — G.L.C. will not move them or rehouse them. They
were rehoused by the council into very bad conditions.
Emotionally psychotic disturbed child — mother apathetic due to
conditions.
Psychosomatic and physical illnesses.
Child mentally sub-normal (due to physical environment, lack of
stimulation ? one of the causes is social conditions).

Case Six

Family of nine.
Living in three usable rooms out of six rooms — density of 3 p/ur.
Place in such bad condition that G.L.C. will not repair it, no bath
(broken), no inside toilet, rotten floors, rats.
Father alcoholic unskilled — couldn't keep up with the situation
and took an overdose — he doesn't work.

126

Mother mentally sub-normal (for same reasons as above).
Children's department pays rent to keep family together.
They will not be rehoused in better conditions.

Case Seven

Family of seven.
Living in one room – divided into three – density of 7 p/r.
Conditions very damp, pipes run through room.
Psychosomatic diseases – children sent away – home broken up until conditions are better.
Stopped paying rent until place repaired – served with eviction order.
Once rents are witheld from the G.L.C. family will not be rehoused, as they are considered a 'risk family'.
Catholic – mother now has I.U.D.

Case Eight

Family of seven.
Living in six rooms at density of 1·1 p/r.
Father unskilled, for first time held job for six months.
Conditions all very damp, no bath, no hot water, no inside toilet.
Can't afford to heat the house.
Can't afford to repair the house – landlords won't.
Don't do anything unless actively helped by social workers and welfare officers.

Case Nine

Family of ten.
Rehoused in six rooms at density of 1·7 p/r.
Father unskilled and unemployed – existing on social security of £19 per week. If he were working the most he could hope to earn would be £14 before tax.
Bad conditions, no inside toilet.
Father gets handouts from welfare officers and sells them – this has landed him in court.
Two daughters leaving home, setting themselves up in flat – both have illegitimate children.
Parents will not use contraception or be sterilized.
Children shoplift – no control exercised by parents.
Unable to plan day-to-day situation.

Family of six.
Living in two rooms – density of three p/r.
Very bad conditions, damp, no bath, no hot water, no inside toilet.
Rooms have decayed to the point of literally rotting away.
Last child, battered baby case.
Mother treated for manic depression – caused by conditions.

The case book proves nothing but implies that conditions do affect those living in the area. The clinics and social workers are overworked in this situation. Just across the road in N16, an area very similar to N19, the area in question, the number of psychiatric patients discharged was 113 per cent of the national average; this was a twenty-eight per cent increase over the two years preceding 1968. Admissions to psychiatric treatment centres have risen seventeen per cent.

Many of these people have been in the area less than five years. The fact that there is such a large percentage of emotionally disturbed and ill people could be related to the pressures that forced them to live in such conditions. Once there, they are unable to get out, or they feel they are unable to get out. Talking to workers in the social welfare clinic, it immediately becomes apparent that the state of the house and accompanying sanitary conveniences is the basic root of 'urban neuroses'. Within council flats conditions are just as bad. As with all other landlords the G.L.C. does not consider itself interested in the welfare of its tenants provided the money comes in. There are many cases of families who avoid the bureaucratic procedures and take action that is in the long term detrimental to themselves. To get the landlord, whether public or private, to act in a positive way is almost impossible except under pressures from organizations and departments involved in the social and welfare problems of those living in the area. If a family, out of desperation, takes action by stopping rent payments, the landlord is quick to reply – but only by evicting, or threatening to evict, the family. It is not surprising that families housed by the G.L.C. will continue to pay rent for very bad conditions so that eventually there may be a possibility of a new place to live. If stopping rent has the effect of categorizing the family as a 'risk family', it is not surprising that people do not want to risk applying for rent rebates, although it is their right. Islington has one of the highest percentages of unclaimed rent rebates in the country.

It is these pressures, the inability to act when circumstances threaten the household, the futility of battling against bureaucratic organizations leading to the decline in self-realization, the dependence on social workers and welfare officers for decisions, which result in apathy and resignation that is part of social isolation and alienation.

When people are evicted or are thrown out by bad landlords as is the case for twenty-two per cent of those who moved into this area, they become the responsibility of the welfare department. These people are rehoused in 'welfare accommodation' (or, as it is called, Part II housing). The conditions in many of these houses are worse than in the original accommodation. As can be seen by the survey on housing and unemployment, many houses have few sanitary facilities, the walls and floors are damp and rotten. Many families who have recently come to live in the area are living in welfare accommodation. To get rehoused by the council or G.L.C. they have to pay off rent arrears which, in many cases, they cannot. Sometimes the children's department will pay the rent to keep the family together. It is these people who are rehoused in welfare housing, much of which is due to be pulled down.

To get a house or flat at all requires the family, by law, to be literally out on the streets before help will be given. Most families who are about to be evicted or who have been given a court order, will stay put until they are physically thrown out. These people and most of those in welfare accommodation, whether Part II or Part III, are priority cases, yet they are not put on priority housing lists for council flats or maisonettes. Most have over 2·4 children on average and are consequently not catered for by the boroughs or G.L.C. As with most cases in the battle of survival, the weakest are left at the bottom. 'Half-way housing' and the general shifting of 'residual populations' from one slum to another (as is the case with many of the housing associations) is common. People are housed in 'deprived areas' which are allocated to the welfare department. Those in flats or houses taken over by the housing associations have very little chance of being rehoused by the council and are likely to be moved to a similar area when this one is eventually redeveloped.

Part III accommodation is for those who don't quite make it, even into welfare housing. These hostels and reception centres temporarily house the homeless. Hillside is such a reception centre. In this hostel the families are not separated and father and mother are able to sleep together. Most families are supported by social security payments; very few of the parents work. Most are under twenty, have married early, or are not married with kids. Most of the families are white (ninety per cent). Black landlords take children, as do most landlords of immigrant origin, because they look upon children as a blessing rather than as a nuisance. Privacy is minimal; 'making love would echo all round the place'. Sanitation is minimal (two baths and two lavatories serving twenty people). Families are put one to a room where there is a man — otherwise they share. But these places are 'taken advantage of'. Families will come from other parts of the country, making themselves 'homeless', specifically to get a flat.

In this context the relevant departments were quite helpful, though showing occasional flashes of ignorance and sidestepping that revealed more than it was meant to cover up. The departments do work together. The welfare department will co-operate with other departments such as child welfare and with outside bodies like housing associations and, within the context, does valuable work helping to accommodate some families in various flats throughout the borough.

On the other hand the prospects for rehousing families were considered good, particularly if there were no rent arrears. Though, as we have seen, many families continue to pay rent, despite bad conditions, for fear of being left out of some future redevelopment, many find it difficult to avoid being caught up with arrears and becoming 'risk families', thus jeopardising their potential chances for rehousing. The problem of what happens with the children and their schooling when the family moves to other accommodation remains unresolved. The mental and physical conditions of people previous to being housed by the welfare department were described as normal, as were the problems with the families once they were housed.

6. Conclusions

A person does not exist without a social context. You cannot take a person out of his social context and still see him as a person, or act towards him as a person. If one does not act towards the other as a person, one depersonalizes oneself.

                                                                    R. D. LAING

Participation and Contribution

'I have now reached the point where I may indicate briefly what to me constitutes the essence of the crises of our time. It concerns the relationship of the individual to society. The individual has become more conscious than ever of his dependence upon society. But he does not experience this dependence as a positive asset, as an organic tie, as a protective force, but rather as a threat to his natural rights, or even to his economic existence. Moreover his position in society is such that the egotistical drives of his make-up are constantly being accentuated, while his social drives, which are by nature weaker, positively deteriorate. All human beings, whatever their position in society, are suffering from this process of deterioration. Unknowingly prisoners of their own egotism, they feel insecure, lonely and deprived of the naïve, simple and unsophisticated enjoyment of life. Man can find meaning in life, short and perilous as it is, only through devoting himself to society.'   *Einstein*

As we have seen, the urban scene provides for greater impersonality and more tenuous social relationships. Some people immigrate to the cities for this reason, but many people within the cities find economic insecurity and personal and social maladjustment. Living in cities can make people more independent and more impersonal in their relationships towards each other. What this tends to do is to rigidify the way we live and the way we organize ourselves socially. Thus personal or group problems are taken over by organized institutions. Bureaucratized 'social work' is part of the urban way of not assuming individual responsibility for social problems, but of undertaking to meet them as a state obligation rather than as a series of personal and communal needs. This social work has become an integral part of urban society, thus cutting more of the few remaining ties with customs of inter-individual responsibility. Person-to-person assistance has gradually died in the urban context until one part of the community does not know, and does not want to know, how another part lives. This applies especially to those more affluent people who are, for the most part, unaware of the living, working, schooling conditions of those in 'deprived' areas.

We have also seen that, with the age of automation almost upon us, and the ease of controllability increasing, 'Big Brother Bureaucracy' has infiltrated to most areas of our private lives. It controls our communications, it controls our socialization, it controls our alienation. It has taken from man human interaction and interfered with interhuman behaviour arising from the relations between man and environment. The laws of conservation state that an increase in anything in any system equals the difference between what has been taken in and what is given out. Looking at what has not been conserved in terms of human relationships within the urban context, whether it is in a 'deprived area' or in the affluent suburbs, it becomes increasingly apparent that the community rarely exists. People are estranged from any decision-making process that affects their lives. They are almost powerless to stop local government which passes as a representation for the local people, once 'the wheels of progress are put in motion'. True, it protects the rights of many. But it has diminished the role of man in the community, and given him a new sense of impotence.

W. O. Douglas in his book, *The Point of Rebellion*, points out that, with the increased amount of information and knowledge about, the 'experts' have so multiplied that man is about to become an automaton, identifiable only as a number in a computer bank. He continues:

Any dissent we witness is a reaffirmation of faith in man; it is a protest against living under rules and prejudices and attitudes that produce extremes of wealth and poverty . . . and that prepares us to think alike and be submissive objects for the regime of the computer. It is a protest against the belittling of man, against his debasement, against a society that makes 'lawful' the exploitation of humans.

The size and unwieldiness of government is increasing, and new channels of communication with people have to be prepared, increasing the alienating effect. A reorganization of local government is necessary to bring the responsibility of decision-making back to a 'grass roots' base, so that 'diminished man' may regain his former potential for 'self-actualization'. Aristotle said that 'the best limit of the population of a state is the largest number which suffices for the purposes of life, and can be taken in at a single view.'

Leopold Kohr in *Economics of Progress* relates this feeling to today's urban scene. He maintains that both tangible and intangible products (such as education) are commodities, which become in actuality 'remedial' goods, where possession, instead of improving conditions, only prevents them from becoming worse. What has happened is that there has been a rise in the level of subsistence, not in the standard of living, so that most of our so called progress commodities have to be produced in such great quantities, not for the sake of advancement, but for the same reason earlier ages needed to produce much less: just to live. Everything, he points out, has a natural size limitation, from a snail's shell to a local government. When the natural size expands, instead of making things better, it produces so many burdens that any increase in productivity, of both tangible and intangible commodities, is consumed by increased difficulties created by excessive growth expansion beyond the natural limits. Social scientists, anthropologists and urbanologists are studying this in the living or dying (depending on your viewpoint) example of Calcutta. There the increase in population has so stretched the resources and services of local and state government that a total breakdown of urban civilization is about to take place. New York seems to be next. This was man's choice of the way he was to live. It now seems for the first time to have proved a failure; careful reappraisal of man's role in the urban community has to take place.

The increased difficulties, he continues, are more pronounced if the increase is in geometrical progression, and the physical structure of the city expands at such a rate that the resulting problems reflect this progression, while the ability to catch up or solve them might only increase arithmetically. Growth is beneficial up to a point. It becomes the principal cause of difficulty once it goes beyond it, and this applies not only to natural level organisms but also to social organisms. When growth does go beyond its natural level something or someone has to suffer. In the case of the urban centres those factors of least importance to the urban scene are discriminated against. The tangible and intangible products suffer. The battle of survival will be won by those who can still have natural control within the social organisms. The size of the city is determined by the function it is meant to fulfil. Once a society is large enough to furnish socio-economic, cultural and political needs, more growth can no longer add to its basic purpose.

Thus there would seem to be a point of diminishing returns, in this case, living standards in terms of the visible and invisible commodities available. The optimum limit is not fixed but modifiable 'in proportion to man's ability to enlarge his administrative vision', especially in the 'size-extending' fields of education, administrative integration and technological development in communications and information. Once this point is passed, Kohr suggests, further growth of the community will add, not to its individualistic function of providing a good life, but to the collectivist function of 'maintaining itself for its own reason'. The individual, instead of being assisted by social growth, is impeded by it. Once a society has become large enough to furnish the individual's social, economic, political and cultural needs in satisfactory abundance, further growth can no longer add to its basic purpose. Human society, unlike biological organisms, grows by unification and integration. Instead of multiplying to keep the size of the state in scale, it has become large and monolithic.

As the population increases, so do social and community problems. The disintegration of overgrowing political complexes, according to Kohr, has to be avoided and this is done by reducing the share of the ordinary citizen's production and contribution which was previously kept by him to provide for his own individual 'substance of life', and making it available to a government whose powers have to be increased in proportion to the falling behind of human administrative ability. The new 'substance of life' is depersonalized and de-individualized. We have seen how it has dehumanized society's needs with the paradoxical result that the greater the social machinery has become, after having outgrown its original mandate both in form and size, to care for the individual, the poorer the individual becomes. The more commodities (tangible and intangible) produced, the less the individual actually gets to enjoy. The effect of this inability to cope with the increasing size and complexity of urban life, on the quest for freedom, results in 'negative freedom': a willingness to submit to bureaucracy, the submission of the self in the hope of minimizing the possibility of failure and maximizing the possibility of success. Not only has man's share of himself been eroded by the 'organization'; but he is actually in the position of wanting, and having no alternative but, to submit his self to the bureaucracy. After all, any failure would mean even more difficulty in controlling the break-down of the city. 'Positive freedom', the full realization of an individual's potential, is impossible under the present system of non-participation, non-contribution, non-communication with centralized authority.

The problem today is that our reduced sense of reality has led to a reduced sense of responsibility and a lack of effective desire.

A change is needed so that people can participate in the structuring of their own lives, where they can make their own decisions and have their own responsibilities; where 'self-realization' and 'self-actualization' can be rediscovered. Government by 'the people' tends to mean that 'the people' or a good many of them should be interested in the way their government is conducted. Few local authorities can satisfy even this weak condition of democracy. Research for the Maude committee revealed most people as ignorant and unenthusiastic about their local government. Many do not bother to vote. There is apathy and resignation at their powerlessness to affect any decisions. But the small unit still survives and must become more important if the increasing alienation of sections of the urban centres is not to continue. The small-scale and the familiar is a protection to the individual in an impersonal world.

In urban authority areas, according to the Hornsey report, approximately three-quarters of the electorate defined their 'home' area as being of a size no larger than the equivalent of a ward; of these, the majority defined its extent as being approximately the size of a group of streets or smaller. The Hornsey report conceived of neighbourhood councils of an average 9,600 people including children, whose duty would be to 'represent the wishes of the local residents on any question whatsoever which concerned them'. They would be able to take the initiative themselves as well as press the higher authorities. They would not have powers of compulsion over persons or property, except for the power of raising money. They would be financed by rates, by charges for services rendered, and by government and block grants from the superior council, which would allow for equalization between rich and poor areas. This would enable them to borrow money, to service loans received, to employ full or part-time staff. The problem of neighbourhood councils is that they exist as an extension of existing local government set-ups. The superior council has the ultimate power over grants and rates and make-up of neighbourhood areas. The rates charged for this service will be over and above present rates.

What is proposed involves a mutual-aid self-help programme on a community basis. The original concept of the community will return. Decision-making will be on a grass roots basis with realized potential for participation and contribution. The potentially contributing segment of society, the redundant and disemployed, could play a useful role, not so much in terms of whether they earn their money by work, or are given free commodities, tangible and intangible, on a welfare service system with active encouragement by the government, but for the self-realization of the potential each man can give to society. Authority will be within their own hands. The community will take decisions affecting its own education, leisure, housing and communications facilities. Responsibility, participation and contribution will be the first step in realizing in action what they themselves can do.

To attain this measure of autonomy without becoming an extension of the already alienating and alienated local government authority, a total reconstruction of local government on a new basis will have to take place. This would be an attempt at the redevelopment of the lowest echelon of the tertiary government system of national, regional, and local governments. Instead of power residing in a few councillors and aldermen a more democratic situation could be set up.

Communities and the Folk Moot

To participate in and to be involved with one's environment both physical and economic can only be achieved by taking away the alienating factors of an overgrown bureaucratically-run organization, such as the local authorities. The Maude report favours the increase in size of 'authority' — assuming (maybe for political reasons) that management reorganization is what is needed to create more efficiency in solving urban problems. The main problem with this solution is that all that has been achieved is greater distance between decision-making and an urban end-product, whether this takes the form of a new park or a complete redevelopment of the area. This greater distance leads to a greater sense of alienation. For those in decaying areas this means more and more reliance on public service departments which tend to be more of a policy making system than a service. People are not involved in taking decisions that affect their lives. The Hornsey report showed that a large majority of people in the area favoured 'self determination' by 'neighbourhood units', whatever political, employment or age group they belonged to.

A community is based on geographical and social parameters. It may be determined by anything from a main road to a catchment area of a primary school. But although a political decision to do

138

this can be taken very quickly, creating a 'sense of community' is a slow process, taking a period of years. Things have been getting slower over the last few years and this has hit the 'deprived areas' of the city hardest. To get over this problem of increasing slowness, whatever managerial reforms take place within the 'organization', it is necessary to take 'decision-making' back to a grass roots level. There are various ways of achieving this aim. On the one hand there is street and community action. This has played a large part in Notting Hill, not so much in achieving recognizable goals but in creating a sense of mutual aid and communal togetherness. In many areas which are less exposed to the media, this has taken place in a smaller, yet more successful way. In the area south of the survey area, street action, set in motion by some of the social workers operating there, culminated in the 'winning of the right' to use a small area for communal activities. The embarrassment of officialdom has been one of the few weapons available in the war of survival. But with an official 'lame-duck' psychology, even this tactic is having few results. On the other hand there is change through slow and compromising government procedures. If a government is enlightened or pragmatic enough to act on social reforms, then the need for upheaval or turmoil is lessened. In most cases, there has been both a (sometimes necessary) violent prodding of the establishment and subsequent legislation. In this case much of the foundation could be set up by street action, with the help of free legal aid organizations, advice centres, residents' associations, care centres and so on. This form of 'social evangelism' may help alter the still-existing, Victorian pyramid. The Isle of Dogs U.D.I. gives a good indication of what can happen when the authority has become removed from those it is meant to serve. All these ways rely on the capitalization of the positive aspects of the existing, and projected, human resource.

The need for 'security' is foremost in 'deprived' areas. People have nothing to fall back on, there is nowhere else to retreat to. It is therefore of primary importance that existing social groups should be protected both in their fight for civil rights, and in the redesign of old areas and the design of new areas for a 'slum population', so that the social fabric of the area will not be destroyed by uprooting, and the formation of 'echo ghettoes' avoided. The community in a sociological sense is a basic tool of social development; just like any other organism it depends on its constituent parts to survive or redirect its efforts to changing aspirations. Community development must have such a body. It is essential to any programme involving 'self-determination' of any sort, whether it is 'self-help' housing or the advancement of education of the group in the use of new properties and the sustaining of the drive for steadily rising standards of living.

But how does the community work? Let us assume that the basis is a 'folk moot', literally a place where folk meet. This would mean that the reorganization of existing resources to better use could take place with the least amount of disruption. The existing borough could be divided into communities not in terms of political affiliations, but by selecting those socio-geographical boundaries that people within the area recognize. The United Nations suggests a series of very small groups, or 'cells', which eventually bind together to form a community of, say, no more than 1,000 families. The 'cells' could be not more than twenty families, about 100 people. If this recommendation were translated into a situation similar to North Islington we might find that a small basic unit is a street or block. Those living in the block could form a sort of tenants' association, and acting as a co-operative force could decide many simple things between themselves, such as turning their back gardens into a common area or having a small day nursery with several of the mothers looking after the children while the others worked. Using this system within the larger community unit, committees set up to deal with the problems of the area could be run by representatives from these 'cells' or streets or blocks so that a broad policy of borough redevelopment is evolved from a grass roots level and not from a bureaucratic machine. (It is interesting to note the role of the T.A.N.U. 'cell' system in Tanzania.) Policy decisions will not be created, as is now the case, *in absentia* of any representation from those affected, but the departments will be called upon to help. If redevelopment of certain areas within a community is decided upon by those living there, the department will offer suggestions, although the opportunity for private environmental engineers to tender plans will be open. The representative will be elected by the community, who are likely to know him, for a stipulated time. In deprived areas social welfare workers and teachers could be elected, as their knowledge of the problems would be useful.

The people in the community could have meetings wherever they wished, with a local communication system set up; whether this would be in the form of general notice boards, cornflake information packets or local radio, remains to be seen. They would have total autonomy within their areas. They could spend money on parks, closing roads, or educational activities. Shop-front 'architectural' or environmental design workshops and advocacy planning centres could work on projects with community leaders as is happening in the U.S.A. In the American suburban communities the local inhabitants decide how to spend their money collected from the rates, whether to have a new library, swimming pool or to subsidize educational and leisure activities. Thus if there were ten blocks or streets in a community, each area of the community would be represented. There would be ten committee members, who with the community representative (who could either live there or be hired as a public relations ombudsman) would represent the views of the community to the folk moot and thus help bring the decision-making process closer to those affected. Responsibility would thus be diffused and decentralized away from the existing role of the borough council. Housing or welfare departments would now be servicing, rather than policy making, organizations.

The folk moot, or local parliament, acts as a coming together of representatives to discuss the common problems of their communities and to establish broad policies such as ways of tackling motorway proposals. Groups of neighbouring representatives could consult on such things as sub-centres, bus routes, road widening, common facilities or amenities that would be unable to be supported by just one community. In London a new G.L.C. could consist of elected members from these borough folk moots.

The economic consequences of this change in local government are not great. The present rates and government loans and grants could be dispensed to the communities on a means test or 'needs test' basis. Thus a community that has very few facilities, or whose housing or sanitary conditions are bad, would get a larger grant from the folk moot than an area that was relatively well off. Block grants would help this process of equalization. Richer areas produce more rateable incomes and need smaller block grants. Because of these disparities, the Hornsey report suggested an average block grant of say, £1 per annum for each person within a neighbourhood. This figure might go as low as 50p. or as high as £2 per head in inverse relationship to the rateable value of the property in each area. The grant to the communities could take various forms: a direct grant from central government through the folk moot to the communities; grants from the existing rates; loans from building societies; or special government loan agencies for long-term, low-interest loans, as in developing countries. Charges could be made by the communities for the use of some of their facilities. An urban motorway could provide a form of compensatory toll for the inconvenience engendered to people. Compensation in its present context means that, should a 'Westway' damage an already deprived area, the rateable value of the property is reduced. Instead of making amends for harm done, this actually creates more of a vacuum and the landlord is the only one positively affected. If, on the other hand, compensation was paid and the rateable value remained the same, the annual lump sum could be used by the community or communities affected much more positively. With part of this money much of the environmental, housing and education problems could be solved. In education, more money could be forthcoming from the community for extra facilities, better teachers with better pay to decrease the present high rate of teacher turnover. Small pre-school nurseries and day-nurseries could be built or houses converted for this purpose. All of this should have been provided by the D.E.S. Instead it grants a very small sum per year for schools in priority areas. If the D.E.S. or local councils won't do it then the community will.

The re-use of existing resources can be applied to this situation. City waste material, much of which is lying around in the streets, on building sites, and in dumps, can be used to construct small communally built and run day-nurseries, with only the minimum expenditure on electricity and teaching. Martin Pawley, in his article on *Garbage Housing*, shows that the movement in the direction of secondary technology is growing. It may be that the widening social gap which results in a 'residual' or secondary group of people, will be reflected by a similar break in continuity between primary and secondary technologies. So it seems that re-use and re-cycling potential, whether in material, organizational, or human terms will be necessary to help solve many problems.

Housing is a more complex problem. The main stumbling block is the distinction between private or public housing. Eventually it is hoped that there will be such a thing as community housing. In that situation, especially in 'deprived' areas, some sort of legislation would have to be brought in, so that a landlord, whether public or private, had to bring his property up to at least the standards set by the Declaration of Human Rights of the United Nations. The present situation is getting worse, rents are going up, unemployment has risen, prices have jumped and the supply of private rented accommodation has fallen, hitting those ineligible for council housing. Investment has gone down and house-building declined. The Government could act by offering inducements to stimulate a non-profit-making situation where self-help, housing co-operatives, residential associations, and consumer co-operatives can flourish. Of course not all families want to own a house and it may be that in spite of the failure of the recent bill in Parliament, those in rented furnished accommodation will have to be protected, and their ability to affect their own life-style by improving their physical whereabouts encouraged. The landlord would be given an ultimatum that he either bring his property into proper repair within the present rent limitations, or be compulsorily purchased. One of the results of rent control is the encouragement of disrepair, so that any control policy should not only enforce repairs and improvements but encourage adequate compensation for improvements made.

Another possibility is that the community will install bathrooms and toilets and repair structural damage or damp, and charge the bill to the landlord, who could then pay it off in the long term with interest, while still retaining the house. The desire to own is instrumental in building up systems of savings such as building societies and loan associations, which increase loan sources for housing construction. The social meaning of ownership has been recognized as so important that it is being used in a number of housing situations which were established on the basis of renting. Co-operative ownership, or community ownership and jurisdiction, permit some advantages of home ownership and also some of the advantages of rental, such as relief from duties of management and physical maintenance. This has the advantage of lowering the cost of housing and giving individual families more freedom within the dwelling. But the big difference is that owners can, basically, control the policies under which they live. They have security of tenure, they can hire professional managers or staff. They can make major decisions affecting the state and maintenance of the buildings. In an E.C.O.S.O.C. U.N. report it was shown that there was a

trend in several countries towards the transformation of subsidized rental housing into co-operatives, after a period during which the tenants were given an intensive training in problems of co-operative management.

In New York 'liberal federal aid' has stimulated co-operative growth, as has loan insurance, 100 per cent mortgages and allowances of income tax deduction for mortgage interest and local rates. Elsewhere unions actively help housing organizations. Perhaps ways can be found to facilitate co-operative efforts to obtain land and finance.

With responsibility come the 'spin-offs'. When a person or community is given a grant, action demands an educative process so as to be able to deal with the problems; what to do with the money, investment needs, priorities, and wants demand in a 'deprived' area a higher level of training and education. This means a gradual understanding of the use of money and so an upward spiral is formed, in contrast to the previous downward spiral of poverty. Responsibility, participation and contribution can work, whether it be with children or adults. This is proved by such organizations as the Child Home Centre, where parents and children from a poor area participated in the building of a centre, owned and run by the children and rented out by them to various organizations at varying times, and used as an education or recreation centre. It is recognized that if the families had a personal, social and economic stake in the buildings, they would not only take better care of their own dwellings but also of the entire area.

Could a 'self-help' housing system work within an existing well-established industrial society? Self-help housing can produce dwellings that by design and size realistically fit the social and economic situation of low-income families. All the concern about dwellings' space and cultural requirements can be resolved if the planner and architect understand the people, their needs and desires. The situation where these groups of architects and planners and the housing departments tell people how to live will be reversed. The community will tender out its requirements and anyone, whether belonging to a private or public

144

environmental design firm, who fulfils these in the best way will presumably get the job of bettering a part of the local area. This means that the community has no obligation to the 'New Housing Service' of the folk moot if it cannot fulfil their brief, but can choose from a range of suggested solutions.

If costs initially prohibit building a dwelling of adequate size, it can be built in stages. If the family income rises or the family expands, so can the building. The family participates, if not in its construction or decoration in some way, then in its design. With increasing inflation, present structural unemployment, and future technological unemployment due to automation and rationalization of industry; with greater leisure time and better industrial training and adult education, the possibility of a situation like this occurring in the economic ghettoes becomes a probability. Those with skills could use them for their own purposes and not for an employer. Builders would help to redecorate or rebuild houses helped by those unskilled and now disemployed. An architect's or environmental engineer's job will be doing something about hunger, employment or transport. Advocacy planning with its lay base and community approval will replace the super-ego characteristics of architects, as will the attitude:

. . . 'We are gods and we can dictate to you.' This may be great for the First National Bank, but it's worthless when people are concerned.

The present unemployment and projected disemployment means that a vast productive potential is available. The state of prefabrication of most products makes a 'do-it-yourself' programme more than feasible. The problem here is the coming together of both men and materials in a co-operative manner, on a 'community works' project, using construction as an 'economic primer'. The role of the school must be to educate the people to a more 'self-conscious evolution', with films and lectures about what they can do about their problems, both physical or otherwise. The labour exchange may no longer be somewhere to collect money but may fulfil instead a retraining and adult education role.

In the U.S. there have been several urban 'self-help' projects. A black co-operative movement took several years over the Flanner House project in Indianapolis, building over 235 houses themselves. They were able to get grant aids and training, and although construction of the first few houses took a long time, the contributed time per owner was reduced to twenty hours per week for sixty weeks. The people involved were not told which house would be theirs. This avoided dropping out. In many countries self-help projects have been responsible for training people in construction work.

Certain services will continue to be centralized, such as drainage. But the other side of drainage, the provision of sanitation, will be on a community level. Other services such as health and social welfare would continue to play a part within the framework of the community, rather than within the council. Those proving inefficient or harmful to families concerned, would not be rehired. Eventually, in the long distant future, it is hoped that social welfare workers as we know them today will disappear. Small clinics could be set up with the co-operation of several communities.

If responsibility is built up from a low level this avoids the continual occurrences where the 'organization's right tentacle' doesn't know what its left 'tentacle' is doing; or when two departments actually fight over responsibility or action or even inaction over some problem. The definition of people as statistics or pieces of paper to be put in the In or Out trays will lessen. Problems will be solved by either a 'cell' or community vote of those living in the area. As the U.N. states:

It is meaningless and not good if the different groups isolate themselves from each other and from affairs of the community. It is meaningful and good if there is a communication between groups, if the different groups are involved in common efforts, or if the better-off make efforts that rebound to the benefit of others.

In this way self-realization may be reached. Bureaucracy will lessen its grip and authority will be in the hands of the community. In deprived areas the prospect of participation with the potential contribution of everyone means a stop to the feelings of powerlessness and apathy, and a move towards a positive mobility orientation. Conditions will get better. If a person wants to improve his environment he has the power to do so. Mental illness and deviant behaviour will lessen. Those energies will be channelled to qualitative changes envisaged by the community with its own means.

After the great European revolutions of the seventeenth and eighteenth centuries failed to transform 'freedom from' to 'freedom to' nationalism and state worship became symptoms of a regression into an incestuous fixation. Only when man succeeds in developing his reason and love further than he has done so far, only when he can build a world based on human solidarity and justice, only when he can feel rooted in the experience of universal brotherliness, will he have found a new human form of rootedness, will he have transformed his world into a truly human home.   *Fromm*

'A cell is a self maintaining system capable of metabolism and digestion . . . intake of substance to maintain or extend its own structure and which in part it rejects as excrement . . . it has knowledge of its environment.'

Kenneth Boulding

Bibliography

A.R.S.E. Publication. Socialist Review Publishing Co.

Abrams, C., *Housing in the Modern World,* Faber & Faber, 1969.

Argyle, M., *Psychology and Social Problems,* Methuen, 1964.

Boulding, K. E., *Image,* University of Michigan Press, 1956.

Boulding, K. E., *Meaning of the Twentieth Century,* Harper & Row, 1965.

Child Poverty Action Group, *C.P.A.G. abridged report,* 1970.

Clinard, M. B., *Sociology of Deviant Behaviour,* Holt, Rinehart & Winston, 1968.

Conant, J. B., *Slums and Suburbs,* McGraw-Hill, 1968.

Faunce, W. A., *Problems of Industrialised Society,* McGraw-Hill, 1968.

Friedmann, G., *Industrialised Society,* Free Press of Glencoe, 1965.

Fromm, E., *Fear of Freedom,* Routledge & Kegan Paul, 1942.

Fromm, E., *Sane Society,* Routledge & Kegan Paul, 1963.

Galbraith, J. K., *The Affluent Society,* Penguin Books, 1962.

Ginsberg, E., *Manpower Strategy for the Metropolis,* Columbia University Press, 1968.

Ginsberg, E., *Technology and Social Change,* Columbia University Press, 1964.

Harrington, M., *Accidental Century,* Macmillan (New York), 1965.

Hoggart, R., *Uses of Literacy,* Penguin Books, 1958.

Huxley, A., *Island,* Penguin Books, 1964.

I.L.O. report, *Employment Policies of Industrialized Countries,* 1968.

Institute of Community Studies report, *Urban Studies,* 1969.

Jones, LeRoi, *Home,* MacGibbon & Kee, 1968.

Kahn, H., *World Futures,* Science Journal magazine, October 1967.

Kohr, L., *Economics of Progress,* IKON, Leeds University Magazine, 1967.

Krech, Crutchfield & Ballachey, *Individual and Society,* McGraw-Hill, 1962.

Lorenz, K., *On Aggression,* Methuen, 1966.

Lundberg, Schrag, Larsen & Catton, *Foundations of Sociology,* D. McKay, 1964.

Malinowsky, B., *Scientific Theory of Culture,* Oxford University Press, 1970.

Mizrachi, E. H., *Study of Anomie,* Free Press of Glencoe, 1964.

National Commission of Causes and Prevention of Violence report, *Violence in America,* 1969.

National Suggestions Centre report, *Hornsey Plan,* 1969.

Newsweek, on Advocacy Planning, 4.4.70.

Notting Hill Housing Service, *Notting Hill Housing Survey,* London, 1967.

Osberkhan, H., *'Automation', Forecasting the Future,* Science Journal magazine, October 1967.

Pawley, M., *Garbage Housing,* Architectural Design, February 1971.

Plain Truth — on Urbanization — Ambassador College, 1970.

Psychiatric Rehabilitation Association report, *Mental Illness in Four London Boroughs,* P.R.A., 1969.

Reismann, D., *The Lonely Crowd,* Yale University Press, 1961.

Tawney, R. H., *Acquisitive Society,* Bell & Sons, 1921.

Towraine, A., *Workers' Attitude to Technological Change,* O.E.C.D. report, 1966.

T.U.C. report, *Automation and Technological Change,* 1969.

U.N. report on *Social Aspects of Housing and Urban Development,* U.N., 1967.

U.N. report on *Economic Aspects of Housing,* U.N., E.C.O.S.O.C., 1967.

'WHEN YOU'VE GOT NOTHING,
YOU'VE GOT NOTHING TO LOSE'
Bob Dylan

" ...SWEPT LIKE DIRT INTO THE CORNERS AND CRACKS OF THE CITY, TO BE FORGOTTEN, EVEN BY THEMSELVES ..."

AREA AFTER 1 year

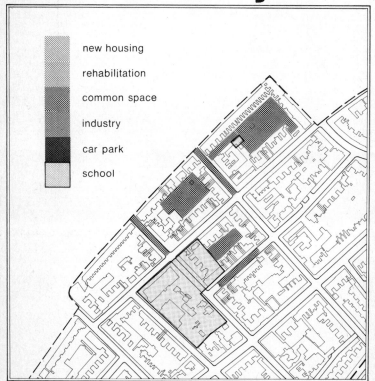

new housing
rehabilitation
common space
industry
car park
school

AREA AFTER 5 years

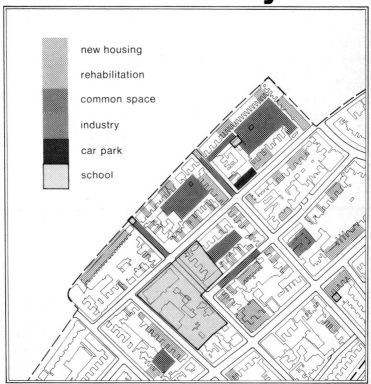

new housing

rehabilitation

common space

industry

car park

school

AREA AFTER 10 years

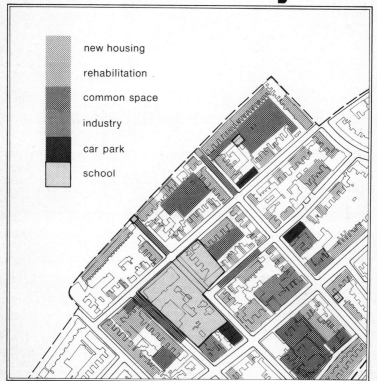

new housing

rehabilitation

common space

industry

car park

school

QUESTION — Relevance of The Case Studies?

Sensationalism — avoided?

Exceptions rather Than the Rules?

Pointers for future s/answers?